Reflective Practice for Policing Students

Policing Matters

Reflective Practice for Policing Students

Selina Copley

Series editors
P A J Waddington
Martin Wright

For my mum, Joyce Copley

First published in 2011 by Learning Matters Ltd

British Library Cataloguing in Publication Data
A CIP record for this book is available from the British Library.

ISBN: 978 1 84445 848 6

This book is also available in the following ebook formats:

Adobe ebook   ISBN: 978 1 84445 850 9
EPUB ebook   ISBN: 978 1 84445 849 3
Kindle   ISBN: 978 0 85725 048 3

Cover and text design by Toucan Graphic Design Ltd
Project Management by Diana Chambers
Typeset by Kelly Winter
Printed and bound in Great Britain by Short Run Press Ltd, Exeter, Devon

Learning Matters Ltd
20 Cathedral Yard
Exeter EX1 1HB
Tel: 01392 215560
info@learningmatters.co.uk
www.learningmatters.co.uk

All weblinks and web addresses in this book have been carefully checked prior to publication, but for up-to-date information please visit the Learning Matters website, www.learningmatters.co.uk.

Contents

Acknowledgements

With thanks to Michelle Hayles and Kevin Gorman for the development and inspirational leadership of the Police Studies Foundation Degree at the University of Huddersfield, and for the opportunity to teach reflective practice to policing students. I would particularly like to acknowledge, with much gratitude, the contribution of Michelle Hayles to my knowledge in this area of practice teaching, and thank her for her kindness and support as a friend and mentor.

1 The police student: an adult learner

Introduction

This chapter introduces you to the importance of reflection as an adult learner. It sets the scene by explaining the importance of adult education for policing students and some of the background to the range of educational programmes that police students receive. The chapter then describes the key differences between adult education and the type of learning that you may have experienced at school. Finally, it explains the crucial role that reflection will play for you as an adult learner during your studies and why it is important.

It is useful to think about what you already know about being an adult learner. We will start with a knowledge check – a series of questions to help you assess what knowledge you already have. At the end of this chapter you are asked to complete this exercise again in order to assess what you have learned.

Knowledge check

- *What do you think the benefits of adult learning might be for police students?*

- *What do you know about being an adult learner?*

- *Why is reflection important for adult learning?*

First, we consider the key developments in educational policy during recent years.

Developments in educational policy

In 1997 the Labour party came back into power after 18 years of Conservative administration. A key aim of the new government was to modernise the public sector, including departments such as social services, health and education. You may remember the slogan 'Education, Education, Education' that was made famous by the then Prime Minister Tony Blair and that emphasised the government's commitment to improving educational standards in Britain. While there is no doubt that primary and secondary schools received a significant amount of attention, the reforms were intended to improve the life chances of citizens at all stages of their lives and therefore included adult learning and education. We summarise the key themes of some of the policies that were introduced in order to achieve this, concentrating on three particular documents that have had a major influence upon the way that adult education has developed.

- *The learning age: a renaissance for a new Britain* (1998).

- *Skills for life* (2001).

- *Twenty-first century skills* (2003).

The learning age: a renaissance for a new Britain (1998)

Summary of key points
The main aim of the Green Paper or consultation document *The learning age: a renaissance for a new Britain* (Department for Education and Skills, 1998) was to improve the general standards of adult education in Britain. The key areas of recommendation were as follows.

- A better skilled workforce.

- Wider access to adult education for disadvantaged groups.

- A society that enjoys learning.

This meant that adult education was to be more widely available within colleges, universities and the workplace. In particular, it would aim to target groups of adults who might not previously have had the opportunity to achieve an educational qualification. Public sector workers, including police officers, were to be included in this group. It was intended that this would improve an individual's career opportunities, and provide the workforce with the correct skills so that they could perform their role to the highest possible standard. There was also to be a commitment to what was referred to as 'lifelong learning'. This term refers to the opportunity to continue learning at various times throughout life, or during your career.

Skills for life (2001)

Summary of key points
The *Skills for life* strategy, launched in 2001, identified that large numbers of adults in Britain, including public sector staff, did not have adequate basic skills in English and mathematics (Department for Education and Skills, 2002).The need for this to be addressed was outlined, and recommendations included a range of courses offering adults the opportunity to improve these skills. It also strengthened the argument for university standard education, because one of the key elements of this is the development of good written and verbal communication skills.

Twenty-first century skills (2003)

Summary of key points
Practical plans to improve standards of education in Britain were published in 2003 within the White Paper *Twenty-first century skills* (Department for Education and Skills, 2003). Its key aim was to ensure that the workforce had the correct skills for employment. The document outlined the development of a network of Sector Skills Councils. Each of these agencies would help to identify the key skills that each type of employee was required to have in order to be competent in their role. The minimum standard of competence would apply to every member of staff in that role across the country. These minimum requirements were referred to as National Occupational Standards (NOS).

The learning requirements for police students would therefore be agreed in partnership with a new agency called Skills for Justice.

PRACTICAL TASK

*Visit the Skills for Justice website at **www.skillsforjustice.com**. Explore the areas that Skills for Justice covers. Then click the tab at the top of the Skills for Justice home page called National Occupational Standards. In this section, explore the area entitled 'What are NOS and how do they work?'*

Developments in police training

The fight against crime

As well as wanting to develop or modernise the standards of adult education in Britain when they returned to power in 1997, the Labour government was committed to improving the whole of the criminal justice system, including the police force, and to reducing crime. You may remember another phrase made famous by the Prime Minister at the time, Tony Blair: 'Tough on crime, tough on the causes of crime.' What he meant by this was that social factors such as poverty and poor education – which might contribute to an individual being more likely to commit an offence – should also be addressed. For those who continued to break the law, however, the punishment should be harsh enough for justice to be done. There was therefore increasing pressure placed upon the police force to fight crime and create safer communities.

For any service to perform effectively it is essential that the correct training is provided – it ensures that personnel have the correct skills to perform their role. The demand for a more effective police force, as well as the specific developments that were taking place in adult education, led the government to look closely at whether all areas of police training – but in particular the initial training period – were still appropriate for a modern police service. We now consider the key events and documents that have led to the current range of police courses and the reasons that higher educational programmes have become popular.

Managing learning (1999)

In 1999 Her Majesty's Inspectorate of Constabulary (HMIC) undertook an inspection of the way that police training is organised. The HMIC is a body that reports to the government, and its role is to inspect particular areas of policing in order to ensure that the highest standards of practice are delivered, and that police performance is continually improving. If we consider the importance of training in general, together with the rapid changes that were taking place both within the criminal justice system and within the education system more broadly, it is easy to see why this review was considered to be a matter of some urgency.

The inspection did not concentrate solely on the training provided for new police recruits; it looked at all areas of police training. This included specialist areas such as fire arms training and promotion schemes such as the Core Leadership Development Programme, for example. The key aim was to assess the standard of all areas of police training in each of the 43 police forces around the country.

Varied practice

The results of this inspection showed that training was a key priority for most police forces but that the standard varied enormously from region to region. This was because there was not a national training strategy that all forces were required to comply with. Personnel who were in the greatest need of training did not always receive it, and others received more than necessary. This meant that staff did not always have the skills they needed to perform their job properly, and often money was wasted.

The need for change

The inspection was critical of police training as a whole and made a series of recommendations for the ways that it could be improved. A summary of the key themes follows.

- *A culture of lifelong learning* There should be an approach to training that emphasises learning as an ongoing process. Staff should therefore have opportunities to continually develop and learn throughout their careers.

- *Training that is outward facing* Staff should be less isolated from the public and other professions. Rather than providing training in police classrooms, there should be an emphasis on engaging police staff with the communities that they will be working with. Educational programmes should therefore be delivered in colleges or universities, for example.

- *National standards in training for all roles and ranks* All roles within policing should have criteria for the level and type of knowledge that people in those roles are required to achieve, and these criteria should be the same in all police forces throughout the country.

- *Professionalisation of the workforce* Recognised qualifications should be provided rather than 'in-house' training, enabling individual staff and the service as a whole to become more professional.

If you think back to the strategies for education that we considered earlier in the chapter, you may recognise that some of the language used there is being repeated here. The police service wanted to ensure that their approach to training did not fall behind the wider changes that were taking place within education, and it therefore followed similar themes.

Training matters (2002)

Although an inspection had taken place that reviewed all types of police training, this was the first ever inspection that looked specifically at the initial training period. Police personnel undergo training courses on specific knowledge and skills throughout their careers. A police officer who decides to become a dog handler, for example, will undergo a specialised training programme to ensure that they have the correct skills for that role. The training programme that student officers receive is particularly important because it provides the foundation that is needed to be competent as a police officer. What follows is a description of the training programme for new police recruits as it existed at the time of the first inspection and the reasons that it has been replaced by more modern forms of education, including degree programmes and pre-joining courses.

The Probationer Constable Training Programme

The Probationer Constable Training Programme (PTP) was developed after the Second World War. Many of the officers who were recruited at this time were armed service personnel who had been discharged from active military service. In a similar way, the accommodation that was used for the training of new officers was often disused military accommodation. It is therefore easy to see why the PTP was delivered not only in a somewhat military style but also in isolation from the general public. There was also a strong emphasis upon police powers and the learning of law knowledge, and less emphasis upon professional attitudes and behaviour (*Managing learning* [Home Office, 1999]).

The PTP was an 'in-house' training scheme, which meant that the skills and knowledge provided to new recruits were delivered locally by police trainers. While there is no doubt that some trainers trained staff to an excellent standard, their own skills and the content of the training varied enormously. The training provided by a particular police force was not required to be of the same standard or include the same elements as that provided by a police force in another area of the country.

One final thing to note about in-house police training at the time is that it did not carry with it a nationally recognised qualification. While a new recruit who had received the PTP programme was, of course, a qualified police officer who could be transferred to another police force within the country if necessary, they would not be able to use their skills for any other type of professional role. For some individuals this did not create a problem because they continued to be police officers for the whole of their working life. However, for people who left the police service – perhaps because of a change in personal circumstances, such as ill health, or because they simply wished to change career – their police status would be of no use to them, and they would be required to retrain from scratch in a new area of employment.

The findings of *Training matters* (2002)

In 2002 an inspection took place that looked solely at the PTP, and the report that was produced was called *Training matters*. There were several reasons why this particular review was considered necessary. These are listed below.

- A review of the PTP had never taken place. In some ways it remained very similar to the training programme developed after the Second World War.

- A review of the whole of police training had already taken place, and it had been identified that there was a need for improvement across all areas of police training.

- Recent changes in adult educational policy had highlighted the need for better standards of work-based learning and education, including basic numeracy and literacy skills.

- The Crime Fighting Fund had been introduced (see below).

The Crime Fighting Fund (2000)

As already discussed, the government at this time wanted to build safer communities by being 'tough on crime'. One of the measures taken to achieve this goal was to expand the police force by employing 9,000 new police officers. All of these new recruits required training, and this placed a great deal of pressure upon the existing PTP programme. One of the key concerns was that training resources such as classrooms simply could not cope with such large numbers of new students. It also did not make sense to invest in such a large training exercise without first checking whether it was still providing the most up-to-date skills (*Training matters* [Home Office, 2002]).

The way forward

The overall conclusion from the inspection was that the PTP was no longer adequate for twenty-first century policing and should therefore be replaced. The recommendations made as a result of this inspection were, in many ways, similar to those contained within the previous report *Managing learning* (1999). The main changes thought to be necessary were identified as follows.

- The initial training period should be regarded as one of the most important ways to ensure that the police force continues to develop and improve as a professional organisation. This is because it is an opportunity to provide new police officers with the best possible skills to ensure that they are highly trained and competent. The initial training period could therefore be regarded as a vital investment that would help to improve the general standard of service provided by the police.

- The training programme should include a much greater element of diversity training. The Macpherson Report was published in 1999, following the Stephen Lawrence Inquiry – Stephen Lawrence was a black teenager who had been stabbed to death in London in 1993, and no one was ever charged with his murder. The Macpherson Report had a huge effect upon the whole of policing because it came to the conclusion that the initial investigation into this case had been deeply flawed. One of the key criticisms was that there had been elements of what was referred to as institutional racism. This term refers to a situation in which an organisation fails to deal with an individual or group fairly or appropriately because of their race or ethnic origin (Macpherson, 1999). It was felt that the new training arrangements offered an opportunity for police students to be given a better understanding of the needs of diverse groups within the communities that they would be policing, which might include people from black and minority ethnic groups (BME) or people who are lesbian, gay or transsexual, for example. It was hoped that this, in turn, might help to restore the confidence of particular groups within the community in the police.

- There should be a national 'framework' for the initial training programme; that is, there should be a basic structure to the programme that applied across the whole of the country. Particular forces might continue to deliver their initial training programmes in different ways, and they would be perfectly entitled to do so because the needs of each force and the communities that they police differ depending upon the location (for example, inner city areas are very different from rural communities). What was thought to be important, regardless of the style of delivery, was that there should be a set of compulsory standards and competencies that all forces must include in their initial training programme and that all students must be able to demonstrate that they have achieved.

- These elements were referred to as National Occupational Standards. All police students would be required to demonstrate that they were competent in each of these areas in order to become a qualified police officer.

The term National Occupational Standard (NOS) is one that you may already be familiar with. It is important that you understand what this term means in the context of policing.

National Occupational Standards (NOS)

National Occupational Standards or NOS are descriptions of the particular skill, type of knowledge or area of understanding that an employee must be able to demonstrate in order to be regarded competent for their particular role. You may remember that the development of NOS across different areas of employment was considered within the document *Twenty-first century skills* (Department for Education and Skills, 2003). Each of the 25 Sector Skills Councils – for policing, Skills for Justice – would be required to work with different areas of employment in order to agree the range of skills that each profession or role should include. These would then form the basis of the educational or training programme offered.

Employees in any type of employment are therefore now required to demonstrate that they possess a particular set of compulsory skills before they can be considered competent in their role. The term 'national' means that the standards for each occupation apply anywhere in the country.

The Initial Police Learning and Development Programme (IPLDP)

The current curriculum for police students is referred to as the Initial Police Learning and Development Programme (IPLDP), replacing the Probationer Training Programme (PTP) in 2006 (Stout, 2010). It covers the areas of learning that student officers complete in order to be considered competent for practice, and it includes a series of National Occupational Standards that have been agreed with the Skills Sector Council for the criminal justice sector, Skills for Justice.

The curriculum asks students to demonstrate that they are competent in a range of skills that are necessary to be a police officer – as you might expect, these include such things as being able to make an arrest. It also asks students to demonstrate that they have what is referred to as 'underpinning knowledge'. This involves having an understanding of some of the social issues that affect people within the communities that the police work with, and involves having theoretical knowledge as well as practical skills so that the decisions that a police officer makes during the course of their work can be made in an informed way. This development is partly in response to the criticisms of the previous training programme, the PTP, in which most of the input related to law enforcement and less attention was paid to understanding the needs of the community or promoting modern attitudes and professional behaviour. It also responds to the very serious accusations of institutional racism made within the Macpherson Report by including a much greater emphasis upon diversity awareness. If you are doing a full-time policing degree you will be concentrating on these aspects of policing.

Another important feature of the curriculum is the idea that it is a 'framework'. This means that all police forces have an obligation to ensure that new police officers are competent according to the NOS, but the way that this is delivered may vary from force to force depending on the particular circumstances. Some forces recruit new police officers and then provide an educational programme delivering both the theoretical knowledge and practical policing skills at the same time.

Increasingly, students are encouraged to complete a degree programme, or what is called a foundation degree, before they are accepted into the police. This is often referred to as a 'pre-joining' course, and here a range of learning is provided that relates to the current educational requirements of the police service. The specific curriculum varies according to the particular course, but in general, foundation and full degree programmes aim to provide the type of theoretical knowledge that will be needed for modern policing and are often designed according to the police curriculum and the NOS.

For students who have completed a pre-joining programme such as a foundation or full degree course, it is possible that you may have met some of the learning objectives required by the NOS in an informal way, prior to joining the police. The extent to which this will be taken into consideration depends upon the particular course you have completed and the police force that you are accepted into. It may be useful to check these details with your particular learning environment. Some police forces say that they favour, or in the future may accept only recruits who have already satisfied some of the under-pinning knowledge elements of the learning curriculum. This way, the police training programme can concentrate upon the practical skills that you are required to learn in order to perform your role as a police officer, and you will already understand some of the wider social issues and the importance of refection. Other forces may aim to provide a wider training package and give credit for the learning elements that you have already satisfied during your pre-joining course. In general, however, employers increasingly favour employees who have a graduate-level education.

PRACTICAL TASK

Before reading the next section, consider the areas for improvement identified by Training matters *(Department for Education and Skills, 2002) and your own reasons for choosing to undertake a degree programme. Make a list of what you think the key benefits of this type of learning might be, from both an educational and a professional point of view.*

What follows is a summary of the main educational and professional advantages of having completed a degree programme. It expands upon the ideas that you started to consider within the practical task.

The popularity of the undergraduate degree programme

The educational perspective

- Providing adult learners with a better standard of education strengthens the workforce as a whole and equips them with transferable skills and qualifications.

- It allows employees within the public sector the opportunity to strengthen their literacy (reading and writing) skills. While an in-service training programme may ask an employee to demonstrate the required practical skills, a degree programme enables students to develop higher level communication and study skills.

- These higher-level skills also include reflection – the ability to reflect constructively on both theory and practice.

The professional perspective

- In the modern world employers favour staff who have a higher level of education, where possible to degree standard. This is true of all types of employer, and it includes the police service because it is usually associated with a workforce that is more professional. If we consider the previous police training programme, the PTP, this is likely to have provided the probationer police officer with the practical skills in order to perform their policing duties. It may not, however, have asked them to do this in a questioning way, but simply have asked them to repeat what they have been shown. With this type of learning it is much more difficult for the learner to adapt to different types of situation or to reflect upon situations in order to develop throughout their career.

- A crucial element of degree-level educational programmes is that they teach the student to think in a critical way. By doing this, the student can learn not only what to do but also why they are doing it. This makes it much easier, when dealing with real-life situations, to adapt, change and think of other ways of performing a task that might be different from the example provided in training.

- The police service recognises that a police officer with a degree is likely to have developed much better verbal and written communication skills. This allows them to present themselves to the public in a professional manner, which can inspire the type of confidence that the police service is keen to develop. In the final chapter of the book we consider how many of the skills and qualities that you may develop during your studies can assist your future employability.

Reflection as an NOS

A very important part of adult learning, and policing in particular, is what is referred to as 'reflection'.

Educational programmes usually include a requirement that you can think and work in a reflective way. Here are the main reasons why this has been included as a key element of your studies as an adult learner, and is also a key element of the NOS.

- Adults learn differently from children. One of the biggest differences is that adult learners make sense of new ideas by relating them to their own experience. One of the most important parts of this process is reflection.

- Being what is referred to as a 'reflective practitioner' is seen as an important part of being a professional. During the course of your professional life you will tackle a whole host of practical situations. Some of these will work better than others and you will undoubtedly learn from your experiences and in some cases from your mistakes. One of the most important things that you will need to be able to do is to reflect upon the things that worked well or the things that could have been done better. By doing this you will continue to improve and develop in a professional way throughout your career as a police officer.

- Similarly, your study skills will develop and improve throughout your learning experience. The ability to reflect will allow you to identify your strengths and weaknesses, and to develop a learning strategy so that you can complete your studies to the best of your capabilities.

An introduction to adult learning

Embarking upon any educational course as an adult learner can be very daunting. Some police students have had lots of experience of adult education, perhaps in the form of A levels, for example. Some of you may have had only limited experience of the classroom since you went to school. Adult learning differs from the type of education that you received at school because reflection plays an important part.

Childhood experiences

Think back to your time at school. For some people this may have been an enjoyable experience; for others it may not have been. There are lots of adult learners who are nervous about the thought of studying again, partly because it is a new experience but also because they have some bad memories of their education. This may be because they did not find the subjects interesting or even because they were bullied. The experience that you had at school can make a difference to the hopes and fears that you have as an adult learner. It is important therefore that you take some time to think about your own feelings about your learning and the experiences that you bring with you.

REFLECTIVE TASK

Think about the following questions.

- *What was your experience of learning at school?*

- *What did you see as the purpose of learning when you were at school?*

- *What do you see as the purpose of learning now?*

- *What do you bring to the learning experience?*

- *What are your anxieties about this learning experience?*

A return to the classroom

An important thing to take into consideration as a police student is that you will be exposed to the classroom environment. As an adult you will be used to making decisions for yourself, you will have developed your own opinions, and you may have responsibilities such as being a parent yourself. Returning to the classroom can therefore feel like an alien experience in which it feels as though someone else is making decisions for you, and this can take a little getting used to. There are, however, advantages in the fact that you have had some life experiences.

Experience and learning

Knowles (1990) refers to some of the differences between adult and childhood learning. Although we consider these in greater detail later, it is worth mentioning here that perhaps one of the most significant is the role of personal experience.

Children know less about the world than their teacher and are therefore dependent upon them for their learning. Adults, on the other hand, bring a certain amount of previous life experience to the learning environment. This means that while you may be learning a subject that you know very little about, you will at least have some life experiences or a basic set of knowledge about the world that you can relate your new learning to. You can therefore think about what you already know, and apply this to the new information that you have received in a way that is much more independent than a child. Kolb (1984) suggests that a key difference for adults is that we learn from experience. His 'experiential learning cycle' is considered in more detail in the next chapter.

Reflection and learning

The process used to learn from experience as an adult is described by Moon (1999) as reflection. It is one of the most important aspects of adult learning and is our focus for the chapters that follow. Reflection involves thinking back to the things that we already know in order to understand the meaning of something that might be new to us.

PRACTICAL TASK

Knowledge check review

Consider again the questions below that you asked yourself at the beginning of this chapter. Compare your answers. What are the key things you have learned?

- *What do you think the benefits of adult learning might be for police students?*

- *What do you know about being an adult learner?*

- *Why is reflection important for adult learning?*

C H A P T E R   S U M M A R Y

This chapter has considered the background to recent developments in adult education. It has outlined some of the key educational changes as well as developments within the police service that led to a range of educational options for police students, and the progression towards university-level qualifications. It has examined the differences between the ways that children and adults learn, and identified reflection as an important part of this process. You should now have a better understanding of the importance of reflection and the reasons that it is a key area of your learning as a policing student.

FURTHER READING

A fuller understanding of the changes to probationer training can be obtained from the full report *Training matters* (2002), available at the National Archive website listed below.

For those who would like to understand more about the changes to police training as a whole, the relevant National Archive web address for *Managing learning* is also listed below.

REFERENCES

Department for Education and Employment (1998) *The learning age: a renaissance for a new Britain.* London: TSO.

Department for Education and Skills (2002) *Skills for life: the national strategy for improving adult literacy and numeracy skills, The first year: 2001–02.* Nottingham: DfES Publications.

Department for Education and Skills (2003) *Twenty-first century skills: realising our potential: individuals, employers, nation.* London: TSO.

Home Office (1999) *Managing learning: a thematic inspection of police training.* London: HMIC. Available online at http://webarchive.nationalarchives.gov.uk/+/http://www.homeoffice.gov.uk/hmic/mlearn.htm (accessed 27 October 2010).

Home Office (2002) *Training matters.* London: Home Office. Available online at http://webarchive.nationalarchives.gov.uk/+/http://www.homeoffice.gov.uk/hmic/training_matters.pdf (accessed 27 October 2010).

Knowles, M (1990) *The adult learner, a neglected species*, 4th edition. Houston TX: Gulf Publishing Company.

Kolb, D A (1984) *Experiential learning: experience as a source of learning and development*. Upper Saddle River NJ: Prentice Hall.

Macpherson, Sir W (1999) *The Stephen Lawrence Enquiry*. London: TSO.

Moon, J (1999) *Reflection in learning and professional development*. Oxford: RoutledgeFalmer.

Stout, B (2010) *Equality and diversity in policing*. Exeter: Learning Matters.

USEFUL WEBSITES

www.skillsforjustice.com (Skills for Justice)

http://webarchive.nationalarchives.gov.uk/+/http://www.homeoffice.gov.uk/hmic/mlearn.htm (*Managing learning* report)

http://webarchive.nationalarchives.gov.uk/+/http://www.homeoffice.gov.uk/hmic/training_matters.pdf (*Training matters* report)

www.bis.gov.uk/about (Department for Business Innovation and Skills)

2 What is reflective practice?

CHAPTER OBJECTIVES

By the end of this chapter you will have:

- gained a fuller understanding of the main features of adult learning;
- acquired an understanding of the principles of reflection;
- considered the ways in which reflection can assist you in the classroom, in relating theory to practice and in the development of your professional skills.

LINKS TO STANDARDS

This chapter provides opportunities for links with the following Skills for Justice, National Occupational Standards (NOS) for Policing and Law Enforcement 2008.

AE1   Maintain and develop your own knowledge, skills and competence.

Introduction

This chapter provides you with an understanding of the principles of reflection. It starts by expanding upon the key features of adult learning and the role that reflection plays in learning from experience. An explanation of Kolb's experiential learning cycle is provided in order to explore the importance of experience for adults. The chapter then focuses on other theories relating to reflection, and a detailed definition is provided. Finally, a distinction is made between reflecting 'in' action and reflecting 'on' action, and the ways in which these types of reflection will assist you in learning in the classroom, relating theory to future police practice and improving your performance throughout your studies and your future career in policing.

It is helpful to start by assessing what you already know about the term 'reflection'. We begin with a knowledge check that asks you to consider your current knowledge. At the end of the chapter you are invited to consider these questions again in order to assess what you have learned.

REFLECTIVE TASK

Note down your answers to the following questions.

Knowledge check

- *What do you think the term reflection means?*
- *What do you think might be involved in reflection?*
- *How do you think reflection might help your classroom learning?*
- *How do you think reflection could be important throughout your future policing career?*

The needs of the adult learner

In the last chapter we started to consider the role that reflection plays in the learning process for adults and the reasons that it is included as a key element of your studies. Here, we expand upon this further and consider the particular features of learning in adult education. We start by looking in more detail at the process of learning for adults.

Some thoughts about learning

We learn continually throughout our lives. As an adult learner currently involved in a formal educational programme, it is important that you do not regard this as the only form of learning that you are currently engaged in. This may be the source of your personal development that you are most consciously aware of while you are studying; however, you will also frequently encounter new situations throughout your daily life that you learn from, and throughout your future career as a police officer you will constantly develop new skills and knowledge, and learn new strategies for dealing with particular practical problems. Throughout this chapter, therefore, the term 'learning' should be regarded in its broadest sense as a lifelong process. We consider the use of reflective learning in specific types of learning situation later in the chapter.

The idea that adults learn differently from children is far from new. Theorists from as long ago as the 1980s have considered the specific nature of adult learning and how it may differ from childhood experiences. Smith (1983), for example, considers several differences, and some of these are summarised here.

Motives for learning

Adults and children differ in their reasons for learning. Adult education usually involves an element of personal choice. As a child you will have engaged in compulsory education as a legal requirement. Now, as an adult learner, it is more likely that you have decided to study, and have chosen your current educational programme in order to assist you with your future career as a police officer. The fact that you have made this choice is likely to assist you in feeling motivated to learn. Adult learners are therefore often considered to be more autonomous – in other words, independent – in their learning. This means that they make personal decisions about whether to study at all, what subject to choose, and how to go about organising their own learning and development.

The need for subject relevance

Related to this is the type of topics that you are likely to learn about. During your childhood education you will no doubt have been introduced to a wide range of learning material. Some subjects – English, perhaps – may have been enjoyable for you, and others – chemistry, perhaps – may have seemed less interesting. The decision to study those topics will have been made for you according to the national curriculum.

This may also be true of your current studies to some extent because the specific subject material will have been decided upon by your learning establishment according to the requirements of the National Occupational Standards for policing, for example. What is likely to be different is that the overall subject will relate directly to your chosen area of academic and career interest, and is more likely to feel relevant to the knowledge and skills you will need to have for future employment.

Adult educational programmes are usually regarded as providers of the type of learning that can be used in practice. Thinking back to your time at school, it may sometimes have felt difficult to imagine how some of the material – algebra, for example – could relate to the real world, or be useful in the future. Now you are likely to be learning the types of theory that can influence your professional work. An adult's motivation to learn, therefore, often stems from their understanding of the practical utility of the subject material and the fact that it has a much more immediate impact on their actions.

Experience and learning

Think of yourself as an adult learner now, and the things that have made you the person that you are. You are likely to have been shaped in part by your upbringing and previous educational experience. You are also likely to have been influenced by the people who you know and the experiences that have happened to you. Adults, therefore, bring a wealth of life experience with them to the learning environment, unlike children, who are learning about themselves and the world around them for the very first time. There are both advantages and disadvantages to this. By having an understanding of the world and the person that you are, you are likely to have a clear idea about the things that you may need to know and the gaps in your own particular knowledge. You may also have an understanding of how you cope best in particular situations. It may, for example, be easier for you as an independent learner to make decisions for yourself about the learning strategies that you can use, how to manage your time and how to cope with stressful situations.

Alternatively, previous experience may mean that you have pre-existing ideas about particular meanings of things, or fixed ideas about how to approach specific situations.

You may also have firmly held values and beliefs that have developed throughout your life. There may be times when this becomes a disadvantage because you may need to unlearn certain practices in order to develop your new learning, or reconsider the values that you have. We will consider the impact of values and beliefs as an adult learner in the next chapter.

Now think about the way that you learn as an adult. It is a difficult thing to be asked to do because learning is usually something that we simply do, rather than think consciously about. As we briefly considered in the previous chapter, children have less experience of the world and therefore need to make sense of situations that they have only recently discovered. Although it is also true that adults encounter new situations, we also have a wealth of previous experience that we can draw upon in order to make sense of them.

An example we could consider here is the difference between an adult learning about a new topic, or an unfamiliar experience, and a young child learning how to read. The child has very little or no previous experience of the skill that they are developing, and *forms* meaning through discovery and continual practice. The adult can relate to things that they already know in order to make sense of the new situation. Adults, therefore, learn through a process of *adaption* in which they transfer, modify and reshape knowledge that they already have from previous experiences in order to understand something new.

Learning from experience: the reflective learner

The key issue that we have discussed so far when considering adult learning is that of all the many differences from childhood learning, the role of experience is perhaps one of the most important. This is an idea that was also presented by Kolb (1984) in what he referred to as the 'experiential learning cycle'. Kolb described the ways that adults learn as a cycle of four stages that the learner goes through. He extends the idea that we learn from experience and suggests that we are able to do this by reflecting upon the things that have happened to us in order to make sense of them. Learning is therefore a process of experiences and reflections upon them. A diagram of Kolb's experiential learning cycle is given in Figure 2.1.

We will consider each element of the cycle in turn in order to understand how learning takes place.

Concrete experience

During our lives we may experience new or unfamiliar events. Kolb referred to these as concrete experiences. This could be a classroom experience such as a new theory that you have been learning about. Alternatively, it may be an event that happens to you in your everyday life, such as having a driving lesson, or a situation during your future career as a police officer, such as making an arrest.

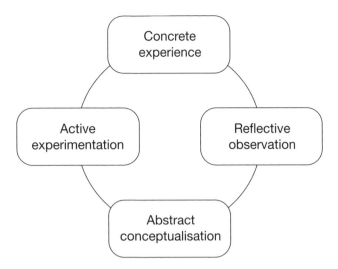

Figure 2.1 Kolb's experiential learning cycle

Source: Kolb (1984).

Reflective observation

During and after the event, we reflect upon – in other words, think about – the experience that has taken place. A fuller explanation of what is involved in reflection is provided later in the chapter; however, what is referred to here is the process of looking back on and remembering all the things that happened during the event.

Abstract conceptualisation

The term 'abstract conceptualisation' sounds very complicated and is explained more fully here. It refers to the process by which we start to make sense of the experience. We do this by thinking about the knowledge that we already have and reshaping it in order to include our experiences from the recent event. We can then form a new theory about the situation. By doing this we are able to learn new skills, ideas or pieces of knowledge.

Active experimentation

Once we have developed our new learning, we start to test it in other situations that we may encounter. The experimental stage is very important according to Kolb because it is only after we have put our new ideas into practice that true learning has occurred.

Use Kolb's experiential cycle in order to think about something that you have recently learned. First, think of an example that you can use. This may be something that you have been learning about during your studies or perhaps something that has taken place during your day-to-day activities. Then answer the following questions.

1 *Describe what happened during the concrete experience.*

- *What was it that I did?*

- *What was the reason for my doing it?*

- *What were my aims?*

- *Who else was involved in the event and what did they do?*

2 *Consider your reflections.*

- *What did I notice about the event?*

- *What were the differences and similarities from things that I have experienced before?*

- *Which parts of the situation worked for me and which did not work so well?*

3 *Assess your learning.*

- *What ideas might I have developed from this situation?*

- *What skills did I use and have these developed?*

- *Are there any new skills that I need to learn?*

4 *Prepare to test your ideas in a new situation.*

- *Would my knowledge be useful in other situations?*

- *Which skills have I developed that would be useful in other situations?*

- *What could I change about the way I did things so that it is better next time?*

Learning as a cycle

An important thing to understand about Kolb's model is that learning takes place as a continuous cycle. Consider again the final part of the learning process, which involves testing out your new learning in practice. When you have completed this, it becomes another event that has taken place. In other words, the active experimentation becomes a new concrete experience. The adult learner can then reflect upon it, consider what they have learned and test it in practice. The learner therefore continues to complete the learning cycle repeatedly. This means that learning is a continuous and ongoing process throughout life.

Defining reflection

We have considered so far that learning for adults takes place through a process of experience and reflection. Kolb's experiential learning cycle has provided us with an example of this process. It is important, however, to provide a fuller understanding of what the process of reflection itself may involve. Kolb considers the reflective element of the learning cycle to be the process of 'thinking about' things that have taken place. By using this as a starting point, we now consider how some of the many theorists have provided explanations for the process of reflection.

The work of John Dewey

Moon (1999) refers to the writings of Dewey (1933) in order to understand the principles of reflection and reflective practice. Although Dewey wrote in the 1930s, his work continues to be referred to in current textbooks that describe reflective activity. In many ways Dewey is regarded as one of the founding fathers of reflection.

Dewey also suggests that learning takes place through thinking about events. He defines reflective thinking as 'The kind of thinking that consists in turning a subject over in the mind and giving it serious thought' (Moon, 1999, p12). In order to understand situations we develop a series of ideas that we link together in order to arrive at a meaning for them. The main reason for this is in order to solve what Dewey refers to as 'perplexity'. Put simply, this refers to a feeling of doubt or uncertainty when we encounter a particular situation that may be unfamiliar to us. It is the confusion that arises from being presented with new and difficult issues that provides the motivation for us to make sense of them. Reflection, therefore, is a way of solving problems so that we can continue to understand the world around us.

PRACTICAL TASK

Think back to a situation that you have been in recently that felt unfamiliar to you – this can be from any area of your daily life. Answer the following questions.

1 What was the situation?

2 Why did it feel unfamiliar? What was different from other situations you have encountered in the past?

3 How did this make you feel?

4 What thoughts did you have about how to make sense of the event?

5 What areas of your existing knowledge were you able to use?

6 What conclusion did you come to?

Reflecting consciously

It is easy to regard reflecting as something that we do instinctively. It could even be said that it is simply thinking about or 'mulling over' events that have happened, and that this is an automatic process that takes place, often without needing to be thought about consciously. For adults, reflective learning is an activity that should take place consciously. Dewey refers to it as an active and voluntary process that takes place using our rational minds.

Automatic action

The non-reflective thinker may observe the following process when thinking about a particular event that has taken place – something that has happened that we are unsure how to respond to. We may react to the situation automatically and decide upon a course of action in order solve the problem. Without conscious reflection we continue to react each time a similar situation arises, and we therefore may not learn anything new from our experiences. The process involves the following: an event takes place; we *react* to it; and we then respond.

Reflective action

Again, imagine a new and unfamiliar experience; however, this time we consciously think about it afterwards. We consider the situation, what worked well and what did not. We then think about things that we could try in order to improve our performance the next time something similar occurs. This time, the process involves the following: an event takes place; we *reflect* upon it; and we then respond.

By using reflection in a conscious way, the learning process becomes something that we can control and take responsibility for as adults throughout our lifelong learning journey.

The independent theorist: learning how to learn

Learning throughout our adult lives takes a variety of different forms. Currently, it is likely that you will be learning specific theories about policing, social issues and the community, for example. In your everyday experience you will learn new life skills that assist you in performing certain activities. You will also strengthen your professional knowledge and abilities throughout your future careers as a police officer. In some of these situations you will be provided with the knowledge that you need – it may be a particular theory, for example, or a policing policy that you are required to follow. It may be that your actions in these situations are reasonably straightforward.

There may be other occasions, however, where you do not have any prior learning to inform your response, or your existing knowledge simply does not fit the situation fully. An example of this may be an unusual crime that you are called to respond to or an accident that happens to a member of your family. It is here that being a reflective learner becomes particularly important. Having been taught reflective practice as a skill, you will have the ability to adapt your knowledge to understand new situations independently. For the adult who can be reflective, therefore, learning becomes a personal process of development. The reflective adult is therefore an individual theorist who can make sense of new situations independently because they have 'learned how to learn'. A series of practical models that can assist you with your reflective skills are provided in Chapter 4.

Two types of reflective practice

So far we have considered the type of situation in which learning can take place following an event. In these cases, the learner looks back on the event in order to make sense of it and learn from it. There will be some occasions, however, when an individual will need to formulate a new understanding of a situation while it is actually taking place. This may be particularly true during your future policing career, for example. It is likely that there will be many occasions on which you will be required to make an immediate assessment of an incident that you attend. Because all situations are different to at least some degree, you may well encounter something that you have very little or no experience of. You will very quickly need to adapt what you already know to the particular situation. Immediate action may be required and waiting until after the event to attempt to make sense of it may not be possible or could even be dangerous.

Schön (1983) therefore suggests that there are two types of reflection. Reflecting 'on' action is the process of looking back on a situation that has already taken place. Reflecting 'in' action, however, requires the individual to make sense of a situation while it is unfolding. We consider these two types of reflective activity according to Schön in more detail here.

Reflecting on action

Here, Schön refers to the type of thinking that we have already considered. He suggests that individuals, and in particular professional practitioners, explore areas of their practice following an event in order to formulate new understandings of what took place, and develop new skills.

Reflecting in action

This is sometimes referred to as 'thinking on your feet' and relates to the ways that individuals make sense of practical situations while they are involved in them. According to Jasper (2003) this process is often automatic and usually takes place instinctively. Experienced practitioners such as nurses, social workers and police officers are therefore able to assess situations very quickly, apply their existing knowledge, and adapt to the situation they are dealing with. This is usually as a result of their professional expertise and repeated experience.

Later we consider some of the ways that as a learner you can use reflection within the learning environment in order to consciously engage with the theoretical material while being introduced to it. Mostly, however, we consider the skills for reflecting 'on' action throughout this book.

CASE STUDY

You and a colleague are called to a dispute outside a high street shop in the city centre. It is during the lunch time rush hour and the area is crowded with people. As you approach the shop you see the shop manager and a man who is in his late teens or early twenties. The manager is accusing the man of attempting to steal an expensive object. Both individuals are angry and shouting. The man being accused of shoplifting suddenly becomes aggressive and threatens to assault the shop manager. You also notice that there appears to be a large amount of blood on the pavement next to both individuals.

PRACTICAL TASK

Once you have read the case study, answer these questions in order to consider how as a future police officer you may reflect in action.

1 What do you think that your immediate concerns might be?

2 What types of information would you want to obtain?

3 What types of knowledge might you use in order to address the situation?

4 Are there any elements of the situation that you might approach instinctively or automatically?

5 Are there any elements of the experience that you might deal with consciously and deliberately?

Using reflective practice

In the last chapter we discussed the development of current educational programmes relating to policing and the reasons that an ability to be reflective is a key learning requirement. Here, we consider the ways that you may benefit from your ability to be reflective. There are three main areas.

- Reflecting in the learning environment – how to make the most of your studies.

- Relating your theoretical knowledge to practice situations.

- Learning how to learn – developing your study and practice skills.

Reflecting in the learning environment – how to make the most of your studies

So far we have mostly focused upon the process of reflecting 'on' action (Schön, 1983). Reflecting 'in' action is often considered to be an automatic process that experienced practitioners use instinctively when faced with complex situations. There is, however, one situation in which the ability to be reflective may be useful for you while in action, and that is in the classroom or learning environment.

Think about your current educational programme and the types of learning activities that you have been involved in so far. These may include group exercises, classroom discussions, presentations and formal lectures. A return to the classroom can seem like a strange experience, as discussed in the last chapter. There may be occasions on which you feel that you have a passive role in your learning, rather like your experiences of school. It is possible, however, to engage with the theoretical material during formal learning sessions in a reflective way. By doing this, you can engage actively in thinking about the importance of a theory and how you may be able to use it in the future, rather than simply listening passively. Not only can this assist in making learning enjoyable, but it may also help you consider the relevance of the material in a way that helps you to remember and learn it.

REFLECTIVE TASK

Consider a learning session that you have taken part in recently, perhaps one that involved a PowerPoint presentation or a taught lecture. Answer the following questions.

1 What did I do during the learning input?

2 What types of notes did I take?

3 Did I ask myself any questions about the material or did I simply listen?

4 Did I think about how the material might apply to my future career as a police officer?

5 Did I think about whether I needed to know anything further in order to understand the material?

6 Did I ask any questions as a result of this?

Thinking reflectively in the learning environment

During your classroom sessions, you may consider asking yourself the following questions while listening to your tutor.

1 What is the theory about?

2 Do I understand it?

3 Do I need to ask any questions in order to understand fully?

4 What does the theory mean?

5 What might the implications of it be for me as a future police officer?

6 What might the implications of it be for a member of the public?

7 Do I agree with the theory?

8 Are there any criticisms or alternatives to it that I could consider?

9 How could I apply this theory in a practical situation?

By asking these types of questions you may be able to start to engage with your learning in a critical and active way. This way, you can start making sense of the material, thinking about the implications of it for real life situations and the ways that you can use it or apply it. The next chapter considers a structured model of reflection by Borton (1970) which may help you with this process.

Institutions vary, however. It is possible that your learning materials may be available electronically via a website. If so, you may consider reading them before each session. This way you can attend the learning session with some ideas and questions already partially formulated. This may assist you in actively engaging with the theories and ideas that you are learning at the same time as listening and participating.

Relating theoretical knowledge to practice situations

Modern educational programmes for students who wish to become police officers require you to develop a variety of skills and abilities. As we saw in the last chapter, the government and the police service itself no longer regard historical training programmes to be enough for police students. Training usually provides the key practical skills necessary for completing particular tasks. An example of this may be making an arrest or searching a vehicle. Often these types of procedures are accompanied by policies or sometimes laws that describe the process that should be followed. There is no doubt that there will be various policies and procedures that you will be required to comply with during your future policing career.

What this type of learning may not provide you with are the analytical skills to adapt to situations that differ from usual practice, or do not fit perfectly with the guidelines. In addition, training may not allow you to understand the social context in which policing situations take place or the types of social and psychological factors that motivate human behaviour. Practice situations, or any social event that involves other human beings, vary enormously. They may also be far more complicated than the examples provided in training. It may also be the case that the policy cannot be applied exactly to the situation when it is experienced in real life.

Underpinning knowledge
For some of these reasons, your current educational programme aims to provide you with theoretical knowledge or 'underpinning knowledge' as it is sometimes referred to. This is to provide you with a fuller understanding of the social context in which policing situations occur, and the reasons why particular issues may arise. This should allow you to make decisions that require you to make a value judgement or use your discretion in a particular situation. We consider the role of values, beliefs and discretion in decision making later in the book.

The role of reflection
The ability to use reflective skills is important for relating theory to practice. It will allow you as a future police officer to assess a real world situation and think consciously about some of the factors that may have contributed to or influenced its occurrence. It is intended that this ability will strengthen your overall skills as a professional and assist you

in making competent decisions. Some examples of the types of factors that you might consider in practical situations are listed here.

- Gender and society's values about appropriate behaviour.

- Domestic violence and the influence it may have on behaviour.

- The experiences of vulnerable victims in the criminal justice system.

- The expectations of minority groups when encountering the police.

- The ways that particular groups have historically been labelled and stereotyped.

- Theories that explain particular types of crime and the reasons that they may be committed.

- The influence that mental illness or substance misuse may have on the behaviour of an individual.

Relating theory to practice

CASE STUDY

Consider the following example of the type of policing situation that you could encounter in the future.

You and a colleague are called to an incident at a family home on Christmas Eve. The house is in a run-down and deprived area of the city that has a very poor reputation. You have been called to the same property several times during the course of the year. On this occasion the police have been called by the next-door neighbour.

When you enter the house you see that a man, a woman and two children are present. Both adults are shouting loudly. There are several broken objects close by. The man appears to have slurred speech and is unsteady on his feet.

PRACTICAL TASK

Now consider some of the theoretical material that you have been introduced to and answer the following questions.

1 Are there any theories that may help you understand the situation?

2 What are these theories and how might they apply here?

3 Why might it be helpful to have an understanding of these issues?

4 What influence might they have upon your actions?

5 How might your theoretical knowledge help you reflect upon the event afterwards?

Relating practice to theory

In the same way that reflective skills can be used in order to apply theory to our professional practice, it can also be used in the opposite way in order to relate our practical experiences to a new theory. This means that it can help us understand a new theory or idea by thinking about the experiences that we have already had as adults and the things that we already know about the world. We have seen that adults learn from experience. In any situation, either practical or, in this case, an educational programme, we bring a certain amount of life experience with us. There are particular skills that we already have and things that we already know. This differs from the type of learning we experienced at school in which we were making discoveries about the world for the first time, and developing key life skills.

We can therefore use reflection in a conscious way in order to make sense of new theories by thinking about what we already know. By doing this it is possible to adapt our understanding to include the new material before we test it in practice.

PRACTICAL TASK

Think about a theory or new idea that you have been introduced to during your learning. You could consider one of the following examples or use something else if you prefer.

- *Theory relating to social exclusion.*

- *Theories relating to the causes of crime.*

- *Communities and community policing.*

- *Theories relating to racism and discrimination.*

- *Experiences of victims of crime.*

Consider the following questions.

1 What was the theory?

2 Did I fully understand it?

3 What do I know about this type of theory already from my own experience?

4 How could I relate this life experience to the theory?

5 What is my new understanding of this type of situation now that I have learned the theory?

Learning how to learn – developing your study and practice skills

Thinking and working in a reflective way is relatively new within policing. Although there will undoubtedly be police officers who already reflect continually upon their practice in order to develop and improve as a professional, it has only been included as a formal learning requirement since the changes to the training and education programme that we discussed in the previous chapter. There are some professions, such as social work and nursing, however, that have been required to conduct their practice in a reflective way for many years. According to Jasper (2003), for example, reflective practice dates back to the 1980s for practitioners such as healthcare professionals. This allows practitioners to improve their skills as they progress through their careers, developing better standards of practice and exploring new ways of approaching situations.

The changing world of practice

Consider the educational programme you are currently undertaking, and the initial police training that you are likely to receive in the future. This will form the basis of the skills that you will have for your policing career. It is possible, however, that you will remain within the profession for many years after you have qualified, possibly 30 years. During this time many things will change, including legal processes, policies and procedures, and possibly social attitudes. It will therefore not be possible for you to simply repeat the initial education and training that you received for the whole of your policing career. Instead, you will be required to adapt and change in order to remain up to date. You will also be required to develop and improve your skills as you gain experience. Professional development, including reflective activity, can be regarded as a process that continues throughout life. This is often referred to as lifelong learning (Jasper, 2006).

There are two main forms that this might take. They are considered here.

Formal learning

The completion of your current educational programme will signify the beginning rather than the end of your educational journey. There will almost certainly be occasions throughout your professional career in which you will be required to update your skills. This is because organisations, including the police service, constantly develop new ways of doing things. This may include the use of new equipment or IT systems, for example. Usually educational and training opportunities will be offered in order to provide you with the abilities necessary for you to perform your role effectively.

You may also choose to specialise in a particular area of policing practice such as the Crime Investigation Department (CID) or road policing, for example. In order to develop the necessary skills for these roles, you will also be required to undertake further training. Alternatively, you may decide to return to higher education in order to obtain further academic qualifications such as a full honours degree (if your current level of study is at foundation degree level) or a master's degree programme. All of these opportunities for professional development are examples of formal learning that you may be offered throughout your career, and they require structured input from other professionals.

In order to make use of this learning, however, reflection remains an important personal responsibility. As was discussed earlier in the chapter, this is so that you can think carefully about what you have learned and think of the ways that it may influence your practice.

Personal development: reflective practice

Professional development can also continue throughout life by taking a reflective approach to the ways that we practise. This is the type of learning that you can take responsibility for yourself as a professional. By thinking back on experiences, we are able to learn from them and continually improve our skills. We can, for example, consider the elements of a situation that worked well, those that did not work effectively, what the implications were, and what we may change or repeat as a result of this the next time a similar situation occurs.

Johns (2009) refers to reflection as a process of self-enquiry which is a 'special quality of being' (Johns, 2009, p3). In other words, thinking critically about the things that we do is a discipline that we can develop within ourselves in order to improve continually. It is easy to see the observation – either personally or from others – that our practice could be improved as a criticism. It is important, therefore, not to consider critical self-analysis necessarily as a sign of failure, but rather to regard it as a positive opportunity to develop and build upon strengths. Jasper (2003) refers to some of the purposes that reflection can be used for. Some are listed here.

- To consider new ways of solving problems.

- To avoid routine practice.

- To assist us in decision making.

- To assist in understanding the results that our actions may cause.

- To develop self-confidence.

Reflecting as a tool for studying

Although these uses for reflective activity relate to future professional practice, reflection is a skill that is also useful for you to have as a police student. It can be used to identify and strengthen your study skills in the same way that it may be used to improve practice in the future. Adults bring a wide variety of skills and experiences to the learning environment. Some learners may have recently completed their school experience; some may have previously been in employment for several years. All individuals are unique, and each learner has learning needs that differ from other people's needs. There are likely to be particular elements of the learning experience that you are better at than others. Some learners may find managing their time and working towards deadlines difficult, whereas others may struggle with written communication and completing essays.

Reflection can help you identify the study skills that you already possess, and areas that you need to strengthen in order to become an effective learner. Jasper (2003) also refers to the following uses for reflection.

- To assist in identifying the ways that we prefer to learn.

- To explore opportunities for learning.

- To assess our own learning needs.

REFLECTIVE TASK

Consider the following areas of your studies and complete the questions.

Existing or 'transferable skills'

1 What are the main skills that I already have? List five.

2 Where did I develop these skills?

3 How can I use the skills I have identified to assist me as a learner?

Time management

1 How well do I manage my time as a learner?

2 Are there any ways in which I could improve my time management skills?

3 What might the benefits of these changes be for me?

Written communication

1 Do I feel confident when completing written assignments?

2 Are there any common themes to the feedback I generally receive?

3 What actions could I take in order to improve my writing skills?

Verbal communication

1 How confident do I feel about contributing in the classroom environment?

2 How well do I feel that I communicate my ideas verbally?

3 Are there any strategies I could consider in order to improve?

PRACTICAL TASK

Knowledge check review

Consider again the questions that you asked yourself at the beginning of this chapter. Compare the answers. What are the key things that you have learned?

1 What do you think the term reflection means?

2 What do you think might be involved in reflection?

3 How do you think reflection might help your classroom learning?

4 How do you think reflection could be important throughout your future policing career?

C H A P T E R   S U M M A R Y

This chapter has considered the key features of adult learning. It has outlined the role of reflection, and a definition has been provided. It has examined the difference between reflecting 'on' action and reflecting 'in' action. An explanation of the uses for reflective practice has been offered. You should now have a better understanding of the ways that you can use reflection in order develop your current study skills and your professional abilities throughout your future policing career.

FURTHER READING

More information relating to adult learning may be obtained from D A Kolb (1984) *Experiential learning: experience as a source of learning and development.* The full reference is given in the references list below.

REFERENCES

Borton, T (1970) *Reach, touch and teach.* New York: Mcgraw-Hill.

Dewey, J (1933) *How we think.* Boston MA: D C Heath and Co.

Jasper, M (2003) *Beginning reflective practice.* Cheltenham: Nelson Thornes.

Jasper, M (2006) *Professional development, reflection and decision-making.* Oxford: Blackwell.

Johns, C (2009) *Becoming a reflective practitioner.* Oxford: Wiley-Blackwell.

Kolb, D A (1984) *Experiential learning: experience as a source of learning and development.* Upper Saddle River NJ: Prentice Hall.

Moon, J (1999) *Reflection in learning and professional development.* Oxford: RoutledgeFalmer.

Schön, D (1983) *The reflective practitioner.* San Francisco CA: Jossey-Bass.

Smith, R (1983) *Learning how to learn.* Milton Keynes: Open University Press.

USEFUL WEBSITES

http://dewey.pragmatism.org/ (for information on John Dewey)

http://www.niace.org.uk/ (National Institute of Adult Continuing Education)

3 The importance of values and beliefs

CHAPTER OBJECTIVES

By the end of this chapter you will have:

- considered the significance of personal values for adult learning;
- explored the origins of our values and beliefs;
- considered some of your own personal values and beliefs.

LINKS TO STANDARDS

This chapter provides opportunities for links with the following Skills for Justice, National Occupational Standards (NOS) for Policing and Law Enforcement 2008.

AE1   Maintain and develop your own knowledge, skills and competence.

Introduction

This chapter considers the importance of personal values and beliefs for you as an adult learner. It begins by returning to the principles of learning from experience. Kolb's (1984) experiential learning cycle is again considered. The chapter then examines the role of values and beliefs in your current studies and future learning and development. Finally, we consider the ways that prevailing values and belief systems are socially constructed, and the impact that they may have for our personal interpretations of the social world. Throughout the chapter you will be invited to consider your own values and beliefs, and the impact that they may have for you as a learner.

We start with a knowledge check – a series of questions designed to explore your existing knowledge. At the end of the chapter you are invited to consider these again in order to assess your learning.

Knowledge check

Jot down the answers to the following questions.

- *What do I think a value or belief is?*

- *Where do my values and beliefs come from?*

- *Why might they be important for my current learning?*

- *How might my values and beliefs affect my reflections as a future police officer?*

In order to begin considering the role of values and beliefs we need to return to the key features of adult learning. First, though, we define the terms 'values' and 'beliefs'.

Defining values and beliefs

The *Cambridge advanced learner's dictionary* (Walter, 2005) defines 'personal values' as:

> *The beliefs people have about what is right and wrong and what is most important in life, which control their behaviour.*

Similarly it refers to a 'belief' as:

> *The feeling of being certain that something exists or is true.*

In summary, values and beliefs can be regarded as our judgements about the things that are most important in life. These shape the ways that we see the world, and have an influence on what we do.

Adult learning: the subjective world

In previous chapters we explored the differences between the ways that children and adults learn. Here, we expand upon this in order to consider the significance of values and beliefs for adult learning. To start, it is helpful to summarise the key points that have been outlined so far.

- Adult learning is generally characterised by choice. There may be occasions throughout your adult life when you are required to undertake a learning experience, perhaps a training event, for example. More often, however, the decision to return to education and the choice of subject will be personal, rather than a legal requirement.

- The learning material included within adult education programmes is usually designed for practical application. Adult learners are therefore often motivated to learn because they recognise the benefits for real world situations and perhaps their future careers.

- Perhaps the most significant difference between adult and childhood learning is the role of experience. While children discover the world around them for the first time, adult learners formulate new theories based upon their interpretation of pre-existing experience and knowledge. In fact, such emphasis is placed upon the importance of experience in adult education that Brookfield (1995) refers to a quote made by the educator Eduard Linderman in 1926: 'Experience is the adult learner's living textbook.'

The needs of adult learners

Throughout the history of education there has been much debate between theorists about the most appropriate methods for teaching adult learners. Chapter 1 introduced one of the most notable writers on this topic, Malcolm Knowles. He makes a distinction between androgogy and pedagogy, and although some theorists consider there to be a degree of overlap between the two terms, the broad principles as set out by Knowles, Holton and Swanson (2005) are now briefly described.

Pedagogy

This term originates from the Greek for 'child' and 'lead' and, when literally translated, means 'to lead the child'. Pedagogy is therefore an instructional model – in other words, a style of teaching in which the teacher transfers their knowledge to a child. The most important things to note are that the teacher is the expert and the child is regarded as a vessel that passively receives the wisdom of others. It is understood within this theory that the child has less experience of the world and is therefore reliant upon adults for their learning.

Androgogy

Androgogy comes from the Greek for 'leader of man' and refers to what Knowles, Holton and Swanton (2005) consider to be the art or science of *helping* adults learn. This model of education acknowledges that adults learn differently from children, for the reasons that we have already considered. The learner should be supported rather than instructed in their learning. Adults are therefore encouraged to take responsibility for their own development and learn in a self-directed way, building on the knowledge and experience that they already possess.

Think of your current educational programme. There will no doubt be occasions when your learning is very structured, such as in formal lectures. On these occasions the environment may feel similar to the conditions that you experienced during your school years – the teacher speaks and the pupil listens. More often, however, it is likely that the activities you are asked to participate in are designed to help you explore new ideas and relate them to your own experience. These may include role play, group discussions, independent reading and, perhaps, even field trips. In this way the educator aims to facilitate or help, rather than direct your learning. These methods are crucial for adults because they acknowledge that adults bring a range of unique experiences to the learning environment. Learning therefore centres upon the exploration of personal and subjective experiences, rather than simply the act of acquiring information.

REFLECTIVE TASK

Think about a recent learning session that you have taken part in and consider the following questions.

1 What was the theory or idea that you were introduced to?

2 What method was used to teach you this topic?

3 How did this differ from the types of session you experienced at school?

4 How did your opinions change as a result of this session?

The role of subjectivity

Here, we expand upon the idea that adult learning is a subjective experience. We start by considering what is meant by the term subjectivity. *The Cambridge advanced learner's dictionary* (Walter, 2005) provides the following definition:

Influenced by or based on personal beliefs or feelings, rather than based on facts.

In order to understand why adult learning involves a degree of subjectivity, we return briefly to Kolb's (1984) experiential learning cycle. It is important to note that, as discussed in Chapter 2, we refer to the term 'learning' in the broadest sense. It applies not only to your current studies, therefore, but also to your future development as a lifelong learner. The cycle diagram is provided again as a guide – see Figure 3.1.

- Kolb's experiential learning cycle begins with a concrete experience. You may consider, for example, a theory that you have been introduced to, either within a formal lecture

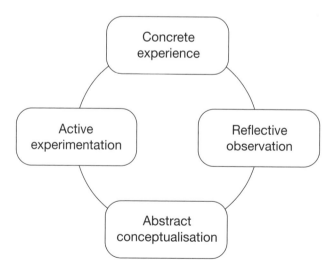

Figure 3.1 Kolb's experiential learning cycle

Source: Kolb (1984).

or perhaps from a text book you have read. It may also relate to something that has happened within your own personal life.

- The second part of the cycle involves reflective observation, or thinking back to everything that took place. This may include your recollection of the key elements included in the theory, and perhaps the name of the theorist. Alternatively, it may involve remembering everything that took place in a particular situation.

- The next stage is referred to as abstract conceptualisation. Put simply, this involves rearranging existing knowledge in such a way that we can accommodate the new information or concept, and continue to understand the world. We make sense of our learning so that it becomes meaningful to us.

- After formulating a new theory it is tested in practice and this becomes a new concrete experience.

Abstract conceptualisation, therefore, has very important implications for the adult learner because it involves the creation of our own meanings. Adults can be thought of as unique and, some may say, complicated products of our own experience. Individual experiences will differ from person to person, and may be influenced by all sorts of things such as class, gender, background and life events. Unlike children who learn in a relatively unquestioning way, the adult learner may bring pre-existing ideas, opinions and even prejudices to a learning experience. The conclusions that are reached during the abstract conceptualisation stage of the learning process will therefore not simply be a matter of accepting a 'fact'; rather, it will involve a degree of personal *interpretation*. It is inevitable that this will be influenced, at least to some extent, by existing opinions about the world and our underlying values and beliefs.

The importance of values and beliefs

Here, we begin to appreciate why values and beliefs play such an important role within adult learning. It may be useful to think of them as 'filters' or 'lenses' that, when looked through, colour the world that we see, sometimes without our conscious awareness. This may be regarded as both a blessing and a curse. Experience provides us with a sense of who we are as individuals, increases personal confidence and provides us with a basis from which to understand new situations. It may also lead to deeply held opinions that act as a barrier to learning unless they are adapted, reshaped or even unlearned. We now consider the works of Jack Mezirow and Stephen Broomfield in order to consider the importance of our values for learning.

Transformative learning

Mezirow's writings have been influential within adult education since the 1990s. At the heart of his theory is the belief that we approach a learning situation with preconceived ideas about the world, and that these develop from the people and culture around us. Indeed he states:

> As adult learners, we are caught in our own histories. However good we are at making sense of our experiences, we all have to start with what we have been given, and

operate within horizons set by ways of seeing and understanding that we have acquired through prior experience. (Mezirow, 1991, p1)

Mezirow suggests that learning requires us to change as individuals (Mezirow, 1991). For this to take place, we must first become consciously aware of the assumptions that we have about the world, and make an assessment about how they may influence our interpretations of it. He refers to this as a process of *perspective transformation* or, in other words, changing the way that we see something. For this to take place we must engage in critical reflection.

Critical reflection

In Chapter 2 we considered the key principles of reflective practice. Critical reflection is a similar but very detailed form of reflection. Brookfield (1995), who is perhaps one of the key writers on this topic, identifies two stages to this process.

- Thinking about, identifying and challenging our assumptions about the world based upon our existing belief systems.

- Thinking of new ways of seeing the world.

Identifying alternative views of the world according to Brookfield may relate to academic learning or professional practice. We consider the implications of critical reflection for your future policing career later in the chapter. Here, however, it is important to consider how this may benefit your current studies.

Values and the classroom experience

Consider yourself as you are now, and some of the reasons that you choose to study policing. You may have very firmly held views about all sorts of issues such as the difference between right and wrong or crime and punishment, perhaps. These may have developed during your upbringing or from your adult experiences. It must be emphasised that it is not being suggested that these views are necessarily wrong; indeed, many of these may be popular views shared by the majority of the public. During your learning, however, some of your values may be challenged, either by new theories or ideas that you are introduced to or, perhaps, by the opinions of others. There will be times when this may feel uncomfortable because our values form part of our identity. What is important is that you develop not only an understanding of what some of your underlying values and assumptions are but also where they originate from. By doing this it may be easier to replace some of your existing views with new understandings. This way, your view of the world can progress and develop during your learning. An opportunity to explore your values and beliefs is provided next.

PRACTICAL TASK

Work with a partner. Individually, make a list of five values or beliefs that each of you thinks is the most important. Then with your partner discuss the following questions.

- *Why did you pick these particular values and beliefs?*

- *Where do you think these values have developed from?*

It may be helpful to think about your immediate environment including your peers, family and schooling. Try also to consider some of the wider influences that may not initially be as obvious. Consider also, for example, the media, cultural expectations or even national politics. Finally, consider the following two questions.

- *Is there any behaviour I would not engage in as a result of these values?*

- *How do I feel about someone who displayed this behaviour?*

The subjective world of practice

Earlier, we considered the ways that values and beliefs may influence your learning during your current studies. As we considered in the previous chapter, however, learning through reflection is a lifelong process, whether this be in a formal learning setting, throughout our careers, or in our private lives. Your values and beliefs will therefore continue to play a very important role not only in the day-to-day decisions that you make as a future police officer but also in the conclusions that you arrive at when reflecting upon your practice. We consider both of these here.

Values and beliefs: reflecting on practice

In many respects the role of personal values will become even more significant during your future career. This is because, as a professional, you will be reflecting independently on situations in order to learn from your own experience. Although within the teaching environment adult learners are considered to be more independent and self-directed than children, during your current learning programme there will be at least some degree of guidance; not only this but there will be a series of formal assessments in order to ensure that you have achieved the level of understanding expected of you.

Although most practitioners, including police officers, are supervised by a manager, professional reflection is a very personal and often private activity. To a large extent you will therefore be an 'independent theorist' during your future career. In other words, the reflections that you have will be a personal decision, and the conclusions that you reach will be guided almost entirely by your own interpretation. It is therefore important to consider the values that may come into play when assessing a situation. For example, you may privately consider the following questions.

- What influenced my judgement?

- Why was this?

- Did I make any assumptions about the people involved?

- What were these and why?

- Where did these assumptions come from?

- If I had not made these assumptions, would I have acted differently?

Think of a future policing situation that you think you might find difficult to address and answer the following questions.

- *What types of situation might I find difficult and why?*
- *How do my values influence the way I feel about this type of situation?*
- *How might I manage these feelings?*

Values and beliefs: interpreting the social world

Another reason for understanding the influences of our personal values and beliefs stems from the very complex nature of modern policing. It has been suggested that our values to some extent govern the actions that we take. As a professional, there will be very few situations that are entirely straightforward and the course of action that you choose may involve an element of personal discretion, depending upon how you interpret the event at the time. Consider the example of a street fight. Even within the law itself, there are a number of ways that this could be resolved. It is intended that your reflective abilities, coupled with your current learning, will assist you in relating theory to practice when making future policing decisions. This is discussed in much greater detail in Chapter 5. Even so, an element of personal interpretation cannot be completely ruled out when assessing a situation and choosing an appropriate course of action.

Consider again the idea that our values and beliefs act as a lens through which we view the world. As we approach the fight, we physically see two people; however, our interpretation of what this means may initially be shaped by all kinds of social expectations. It may, for example, make some difference that the people involved are women rather than men, or children rather than adults. The fact that the disturbance is taking place within a very affluent suburb rather than a run-down inner city area may also shape your judgement. You may also have some prior knowledge of the area in which the fight is taking place. Underlying our interpretations are all sorts of ideas, often referred to as social 'norms', that govern the things that we consider to be acceptable behaviour. It may be generally expected, for example, that women are gentler and more passive than men, and therefore less likely to be involved in aggressive situations under normal circumstances.

The distinction between automatic assumptions and skilful assessment must be made. Of course, police officers assess complicated situations based upon their skills and experience; it is, indeed, part of their role to do so, and is associated with the ability to reflect in action.

Also, it would be foolish, or even impossible, to expect that any individual could approach a situation or reflect upon it afterwards in a way that is entirely objective or value free. What is important, however, is that as a learner (and, indeed, as a future police officer) you have the opportunity to explore what some of your most important values and beliefs are, where they originate from, and the ways that they may influence the judgements that you make.

Read through a recent newspaper and pick an article that you feel strongly about. If you wish, you may prefer to visit a website such as:

- *BBC News at: http://www.bbc.co.uk/news/;*
- *The Guardian online: www.guardian.co.uk/.*

List your answers to the following questions.

1 *What are the key elements of this article?*

2 *Why do I feel strongly about it?*

3 *How has my upbringing influenced my views on this situation?*

4 *What are the wider social views about this issue?*

5 *How do they affect my own views?*

The social construction of meaning

Although social constructionism is a complicated idea, it is useful to consider the basic principles of it here. This is because it provides an understanding of how broader social truths and individual belief systems come into existence. Put simply, there are two broad philosophical approaches to our understanding of what can be known about the world. The first suggests that there are universal truths about which we can be certain. The second believes that meanings are merely interpretations of the world, and that these are created by societies and the individuals within them. Let us carefully consider these in turn.

The natural sciences

At some point during your adult life, you may have heard this riddle: 'If a tree falls in the forest and no one is around to hear it, does it make a sound?' The answer to this is often regarded as little more than a matter of common sense: yes, of course. The reason why this may be regarded as an unproblematic answer is, as Dyson and Brown (2005) suggest, that within the natural sciences there are particular things that are regarded as a 'scientific fact'. In other words, there is an external reality in which certain things are simply true, and can be measured in a scientific way. These facts continue to be true, regardless of whether or not they are observed by humans. It is evident from the study of physics that a heavy object falls to the ground with a thud. Therefore when a tree falls, we do not need to be present to know that it will make a sound. The same principle may be applied when thinking about an uninhabited island, for example. Even without witnesses, it is a simple matter of fact that the sun continues to set and the moon will rise. The understanding that the world consists of objective or factual truths is a type of philosophy referred to as realism. It can be thought of as a doctrine that sees all things as real. The ability for these things or truths to be measured in a scientific way is referred to as positivism. If it is easier, think of this term as meaning that there are things that we can feel sure or 'positive' about.

If we briefly return to the types of learning that you experienced at school, it is possible to consider some examples of this. The function of primary and secondary education according to the instructional model is often to teach children about the rules and workings of the world. You will no doubt have been required to learn particular facts within a broad range of topics such as mathematics, physics and chemistry. Many of these will not have required much, if any interpretation.

The social sciences

The belief that certain things are absolutely true becomes more difficult when we apply it to social theories rather than the natural sciences. It is likely that you are exploring some of these theories during your current studies. Many commentators such as Burr (2003) believe that there cannot be one single truth that applies to all people and communities but rather that there are several different truths. This is because our beliefs about acceptable human behaviour are *created* within societies rather than *discovered* by them, and societies throughout the world vary enormously. At the heart of this philosophy is the understanding that meanings are 'socially constructed' – in other words, made by people. Social reality is therefore made up of a series of subjective beliefs rather than objective facts. There are two key arguments that support this view, Burr suggests: culture and history.

Culture

There are many social understandings that cannot be regarded as universally true because they vary according the culture in which they are understood. It is reasonable to assume that if there were a single 'truth', it would remain the same regardless of the country in which it is experienced. A useful example is the way that different societies view children. In England the legal age at which a child can be held responsible for criminal actions is ten years old (Capriani, 2009). This is due to our understanding about the moral development of a child. A ten-year-old child, it is believed, is capable of making the distinction between right and wrong. Perhaps the most famous example of this is the case of Robert Thompson and Jon Venables, who were convicted of murdering James Bulger when they were ten. Because of their age, and our beliefs about the age of criminal responsibility enshrined within the law, the trial for both children took place within an adult court.

Other countries, however, do not share this belief about the age of criminal responsibility. In Brazil, for example, the age is set at 12 and in Australia it is 14. It could be argued, therefore, that even something as important as the age of human moral development is a matter of cultural opinion rather than fact.

PRACTICAL TASK

If you can, read a short section of a book about a different culture. It may be possible to talk to someone that you know or another member of your learning group who comes from a different cultural background. Consider the following questions.

PRACTICAL TASK *continued*

- *Are there any differences in cultural values or belief systems?*

- *What, if any, are the differences in social practices in this particular cultural group that result from these beliefs?*

- *How might these be viewed within British culture and why?*

History

Similarly, the values of a society change and develop throughout the course of history. Stout (2010) considers the example of the changing role of women in British society and, in particular, in the police service. He suggests that there was a time when only men were permitted to become police officers because of the social belief that men were mentally and physically more able than women. This was not only a socially constructed view of gender differences but one that history has proved to be completely incorrect. It is now culturally and legally accepted that women are perfectly capable of undertaking almost identical policing roles to men.

PRACTICAL TASK

Talk to someone from an older generation than your own. This may be a parent or guardian or perhaps one of your tutors. If they are happy to do so, ask them about some of the social values and practices from when they were younger. You may also ask them how social practices or even legal progresses have changed. Then reflect upon the following questions.

- *How might my values and beliefs have differed if these social practices were still common?*

- *How might my expectations of acceptable behaviour for particular groups have been different?*

You may wish to consider these questions in relation to women, children or individuals from different sexual orientation, perhaps.

Social values and personal interpretation

Although it is not the primary focus of this book, you may wish to read more about socially constructed ideas and how they can lead to stereotypes and social discrimination. *Equality and diversity in policing* (Stout, 2010), another book in this series, is recommended. The full reference is listed at the end of the chapter. The main intention of this chapter is to assist you in starting to consider how our everyday meanings are arrived at, and the influence that they have on the way we interpret the social world at a personal level. This way it is possible to consider their impact on our learning and the broader value judgements that we make.

Critical reflection and transformative learning

Finally, we return to the work of Mezirow (2005) and Brookfield (1995). Mezirow suggests that successful learning requires us to change or transform our assumptions about the world, and in order to achieve this we should engage in critical reflection. Brookfield believes that this involves exploring the basis of our values and beliefs so that we can view the world differently. Throughout this chapter, we have explored the possibility that our values and beliefs develop at a variety of levels.

It is possible to think of this as being similar to the layers of an onion. While there is no doubt that our values and beliefs are shaped by our individual experiences, they may be further influenced by the people around us – our families and peers, for example, or perhaps the media. However, there is also a deeper level at which belief systems and values are sewn into the fabric of society. These 'social norms' are specific to a particular culture, and may change during the course of history.

When exploring the basis of our own values it is therefore helpful to consider not only our own personal background and experience but also some of the wider social conventions that shape our understandings. It may be that you already have some experience of this from your current studies. It should be emphasised that this does not mean that all social values should be regarded as incorrect. Many of our legal processes have developed as a result of social values for important reasons – the protection of vulnerable people, for example. The key thing is to begin to recognise that social conventions operate at a deep and sometimes unconscious level and to consider how these influence our own personal values and belief systems. By doing this it may be possible to make the personal transformations necessary for lifelong learning.

REFLECTIVE TASK

Knowledge check review

Consider again the answers to the following questions in order to assess your learning during this chapter.

- *What do I think a value or belief is?*

- *Where do my values and beliefs come from?*

- *Why might they be important for my current learning?*

- *How might my values and beliefs affect my reflections as a future police officer?*

C H A P T E R   S U M M A R Y

This chapter has considered the significance of values and beliefs for your current learning and your future policing career. It has considered the ways that values and beliefs are constructed within society, and the implications of them for personal interpretations of the social world. The chapter has also provided a range of exercises designed to assist you in exploring your personal values. You should now have a better understanding of the influence of values and beliefs for learning through reflection.

FURTHER READING

Burr (2003) *Social constructionism* is an accessible introduction to the key principles of social constructionism. It is particularly useful for students who wish to understand the cultural and historical development of social ideas in greater detail.

Chapter 3 of Stout (2010) *Equality and diversity in policing* considers the social construction of discrimination, and is a useful expansion on ideas of the construction of values.

REFERENCES

Brookfield, S (1995) Adult learning: an overview, in Tuinjman, A (ed) *International encyclopedia of education*. Oxford: Pergamon Press.

Burr, V (2003) *Social constructionism*, 2nd edition. Hove: Routledge.

Capriani, D (2009) *Children's rights and the minimum age of criminal responsibility: a global perspective*. Farnham: Ashgate Publishing.

Dyson, S and Brown, B (2005) *Social theory and applied health research.* Maidenhead: McGraw-Hill Education.

Knowles, M, Holton, E and Swanson, R (2005) *The adult learner: the definitive classic in adult education and human resources development*. London: Elsevier.

Kolb, D A (1984) *Experiential learning: experience as a source of learning and development.* Upper Saddle River NJ: Prentice Hall.

Mezirow, J (1991) Transformative learning theory, in Mezirow, J, Taylor, E and associates (eds) *Transformative learning in practice: insights from community, workplace, and higher education*. San Francisco CA: Jossey-Bass.

Stout, B (2010) *Equality and diversity in policing.* Exeter: Learning Matters.

Walter, E (2005*) Cambridge advanced learner's dictionary.* Cambridge: Cambridge University Press.

4 Models of reflection: a practical guide

CHAPTER OBJECTIVES

By the end of this chapter you will have:

- explored some of the principles of reflection;
- considered a range of models of reflection;
- practised reflection using a series of examples.

LINKS TO STANDARDS

This chapter provides opportunities for links with the following Skills for Justice, National Occupational Standards (NOS) for Policing and Law Enforcement 2008.

AE1   Maintain and develop your own knowledge, skills and competence.

Introduction

This chapter expands upon your knowledge of reflective practice. It considers reflective activity as a skill that can assist your learning and future professional development. It starts by considering some of the principles of reflection. A very simple model entitled Borton's developmental framework (1970) is then introduced and recommended. Some examples of the various ways that Borton's model can be used to assist your learning are provided. The chapter then introduces a more detailed version of Borton's model of reflection that is presented by Driscoll (2000). Finally Gibbs's (1988) reflective model is introduced.

It is helpful to start by assessing your existing reflective skills. In this chapter we begin with a skills assessment. At the end of the chapter you are invited to consider these questions again in order to assess what you have learned, and how your reflective skills have improved.

PRACTICAL TASK

Reflective skills assessment

Note down your answers to the following questions. You will be invited to consider these again at the end of the chapter in order to assess your learning.

1 How reflective am I as a learner?

2 When could I reflect 'on' my actions?

3 Are there any occasions when I could reflect 'in' action?

4 What models of reflection have I heard of?

Principles of reflection

Reflection as a conscious activity

Previous chapters have considered some of the principles of adult learning, and the importance of reflection for learning from experience was identified. As an adult, you may consider yourself to be someone who takes a reflective approach to your learning. You may already think back to events that have taken place during your studies and consider areas that could be developed or improved. Equally, you may instinctively reflect upon events that have taken place within your personal life. The theories that we have considered so far, however, describe reflective activity as being something more than simply thinking about events that have taken place, and rather a conscious and systematic process that involves planning future actions. It is therefore a process of active decision making (Jasper, 2006). By using reflective practice in this way, it is possible to continually develop and improve our skills throughout our careers by considering the things that we could have done differently (Driscoll, 2000). In this chapter we consider some tools that can help you to reflect in a structured, problem-solving way. This is so that instead of simply 'mulling over' events that have taken place, you are able to make an assessment of your own performance and identify opportunities for improvement. Reflective practice then becomes a skill that can be used in order to assist your own learning throughout your professional life.

Reflection as a tool for self-improvement

Jasper (2006) suggests that reflection is a process of self-examination or assessment. As we briefly discussed in Chapter 2, analysing your own behaviour can sometimes be an uncomfortable process because it can feel as though you are being asked to criticise yourself. You may, indeed, conclude on some occasions that you could have dealt with things more effectively than you did at the time. It is therefore important to make the distinction here between self-criticism and self-development. Criticising ourselves is usually a negative process concerned with finding fault or apportioning blame. It is more constructive to view reflective activity as a tool for continual self-improvement. We take a balanced view in which we celebrate our strengths and identify our developmental opportunities. It is usually the case that we are better at certain things than others, or simply more experienced in dealing with particular situations. Reflection should therefore not be regarded as a process of identifying failures but rather as a tool that can assist us in identifying both our strengths and our weaknesses in a measured way, in order to learn from our experiences, and continue to develop throughout our adult lives.

Learning as a personal responsibility

We have also considered adult learning as a more autonomous (independent) process. During your current studies it is likely that you are required to take responsibility for your own learning to a much larger extent than during your childhood. In your future role as a police officer the ability to manage your own development using reflective activity will be entirely your own responsibility. This is less problematic for practitioners such as nurses or social workers because their organisations require them to perform reflective activity as part of their duties. Formal arrangements are therefore usually made to allow for this, often in the form of journal writing or an activity referred to as 'clinical supervision'. In Chapter 7 we consider the ways that you too may be able to use a reflective journal.

Clinical supervision is referred to by Johns (2009) as a process involving the development of a relationship between a worker and a supervisor. The supervisor assists the member of staff in thinking critically about their performance by asking them the types of question contained within each stage of a reflective model. We consider some of these in the next section of the chapter. The process becomes similar in some ways to counselling because the supervisor can ask the worker to expand upon particular points, and help them to make sense of their thoughts and feelings.

As a police student, it is not usually considered necessary for you to have access to this type of activity. Equally, the structures for clinical supervision do not currently exist within the police service. It is therefore very unlikely that you will be required to take part in this on a formal basis when you begin your policing career, and reflective practice will be a personal and self-directed activity for you. In Chapter 6 a range of techniques that may assist you in adopting a reflective way of life are suggested. Here, we introduce a range of tools that are often used in order to assist the adult learner when reflecting. Unlike some professionals who have been required to be reflective learners for many years, it is likely that reflection will be a new concept for you, and starting to think in a reflective way may feel daunting at first. It is therefore useful to begin by introducing a very quick and easy reflective model that can help you get started.

Models of reflection

Borton's developmental framework

A very simple model of reflection was devised within the field of education by Borton (1970). Although this is a relatively old reflective tool, it is perhaps the most straightforward and is therefore ideal for students who are new to reflective activity. It has also been used as the basis for many recent models such as Driscoll's reflective cycle, which will be considered later in the chapter.

Borton's model was originally designed for practitioners who deal with what are often very complicated real-life situations, and was intended to assist them in tackling practical problems and identify solutions (Jasper, 2003). One of the strengths of the model is that it is relatively simple to use, and can be remembered easily. Reflecting using this model can therefore become second nature to you very quickly. Because of the broad interpretation of each stage of the cycle, however, it is possible to increase the level of critical analysis as you become more experienced and confident as a reflector. You are asked three basic questions.

- What?

- So what?

- Now what?

Borton (1970, p93) refers to the purpose of this model in the following way.

> *It provides an organised way of increasing awareness (what?), evaluating intention (so what?), and experimenting with new behaviour (now what?).*

Here, we consider each of these questions in turn in order to demonstrate how they may be used to structure your reflections.

What?
The first part of the process involves thinking about a situation in its entirety, in order to recall everything that happened. This is essentially your *assessment* of the event. Therefore you are likely to ask yourself 'what?' types of questions. Jasper (2003) suggests that this could include some of the following.

- What took place?

- What did I do?

- What was the outcome?

So what?
The second stage allows you to understand the meaning or importance of the event. You are formulating your *analysis* of the situation, so that you can create your own theory about it. Perhaps the best way to think of this is that you are considering the meaning of the situation and implications of it for you. Again, Jasper (2003) provides some examples of the types of question that you might ask yourself.

- So what were the effects of my actions?

- So what would I repeat in a similar situation?

- So what might I have changed?

Now what?

Once you have come to an understanding of the meaning of a particular experience, you go on to the final stage of the model, which is to plan your future actions. It is important to think about the things that you intend to do as a result of your learning from the event. While planning your actions you should consider alternative options and compare them with each other. The model is very useful in this respect because it allows you to consider what the *consequences* of each potential future action might be, and therefore make a thorough assessment of the best course of action to take. Jasper (2003) suggests the following types of questions.

- Now what could I do to improve in the future?

- Now what will I do differently?

- Now what might the consequences of this be?

By using this model as a framework it is possible to consider both the positive and negative aspects of a situation and the actions that were taken. There may be some occasions when you feel satisfied with the outcome, and conclude that you would not have done anything differently. When considering the 'now what?' component of the cycle, there may be some occasions where you therefore choose to ask questions such as the following.

- Now what successful elements of the experience could I repeat in a similar situation?

- Now what skill did I demonstrate that might be useful in a future situation?

The use of a balanced process in which you consider both your strengths and your weaknesses in the way that you addressed a particular situation will allow you not only to develop the skills that you may be lacking but also to identify, maintain and improve the skills that you already have. It is important, however, that you continue to consider the consequences of repeating a particular behaviour in order to ensure that it could be appropriate in other types of situation.

CASE STUDY

Simon was a police studies student at a university. He had recently started the first year of his studies and had yet to complete any of his assignments. He had an examination and two essays that were due to be submitted in one week's time. Simon felt unsure about what was expected of him for both of the assignments but was more confident about the examination. He felt embarrassed about asking for help because he did not wish to admit that he was finding it difficult to understand some of the theoretical material. As a result Simon decided to leave the assignments until after his exam revision and completed them both immediately before the hand-in date, without seeking any assistance. Simon passed his examination with a B grade, and achieved a D grade pass for one of his assignments, but failed his final piece of work. On receiving his results Simon decided to reflect upon the study skills that he had employed. He therefore asked himself the following questions: What? So what? Now what?

CASE STUDY *continued*

Here is Simon's response.

What?

I am a student who is new to university work and I do not always feel confident when I am writing essays. During my first set of assignments I avoided some of my work and did not complete it until the last minute. As a result of this I did not achieve the standard that I think I am capable of and I have failed one of my assignments.

So what?

I have realised that when I feel nervous about an assignment I tend to avoid it. This could cause a problem for my future studies because if I do not allow enough time to complete my work I will continue to achieve poor grades, and I may not complete my degree programme. I sometimes struggle with essays; however, I feel that I am good at examinations because I have had lots of experience of them in the past.

Now what?

I have decided to construct a study plan to help me organise my time more effectively. In the future I will plan to start my essays much earlier so that I can read through all of my lecture notes and the electronic material that is available. When I feel that I understand as much as I can, I will arrange a personal tutorial. I could see my tutor before I start reading; however, if I do this, I may continue to feel self-conscious about not fully understanding the material. It will probably be more sensible for me to start my essays at least one month before the submission date and meet with my tutor after I have started. This way I may be starting to feel more confident. I am happy with my examination mark but will try to aim for an A grade next time by starting my revision one week earlier.

REFLECTIVE TASK

Using the example above to guide you, think of a recent situation during your current studies. It may be a sudden event such as an incident in the classroom. Alternatively, you may think about an approach that you took to a particular aspect of your studies over a period of time. Think about or write down your thoughts in relation to the 'What?' 'So what?' and 'Now what?' questions of Borton's reflective cycle.

What?

Consider your assessment of the event by asking yourself what happened, what you did and what the outcome was. Try to remember as much of the event as you can. You may also wish to consider your feelings during this period, and the ways that they may have influenced your actions.

So what?

Think about your analysis of the event by asking yourself what it meant and what the implications of it were for you. Consider the effects of your actions, either good or bad, and anything you might have done differently.

Now what?

Finally, consider what you plan to do in future situations as a result of your assessment and analysis of the event. You may make a mental note of this or write a structured action plan. Consider the various options that you have in relation to your potential future actions and what the implications of each of these would be.

Uses for Borton's model

This reflective model is a particularly useful tool because once you have become familiar with the questions 'What? So what? Now what?' you can carry them around in your head as shorthand wherever you happen to be, and because of its simplicity, the model can easily be adapted for use in a variety of different ways. In Chapter 2 we considered the distinction between reflecting in action, and reflecting on action referred to by Schön (1983). We also explored some of the possible uses for reflection. These were as follows.

- Reflecting in the learning environment – how to make the most of your studies.

- Relating your theoretical knowledge to practice situations.

- Learning how to learn – developing your study and practice skills.

Here, we consider these again in order to explore the ways that Borton's model of reflection may be applied. We start by considering Borton's model for reflecting in action.

Reflecting in action: the portable model

The main focus of this book is to consider the ways that reflective activity can assist your learning through reflecting 'on' action. Schön (1983), however, suggests that adult learners also reflect 'in' action. This process involves 'thinking on your feet' while dealing with a situation. As Jasper (2003) suggests, this often involves using the types of instinctive knowledge that we have developed through professional practice, and applying it unconsciously. It is possible, however, to think consciously about situations as they are taking place. This may be particularly useful when dealing with incidents that are unfamiliar and that require you to think very carefully but very quickly about what to do next. Because of the simplicity of Borton's model, it can be remembered and used very easily. It is therefore possible to consider it to be a portable model that can be used during a situation as well as after it. We consider three examples here.

- Reflecting while learning.

- Reflecting in a classroom situation.

- Reflecting in practice.

Reflecting while learning

In Chapter 2 we considered the use of reflection 'in' action for actively engaging with the material that you are learning. The advantage of this is that it allows you to consider the importance of a theory in an active way during your learning sessions. Not only does this make learning enjoyable but it also helps you to understand and remember it more easily. We return to the examples of the types of reflective questions you may ask that were considered in Chapter 2, in the section 'Reflecting in the learning environment – how to make the most of your studies', but here we consider them in relation to Borton's reflective model.

- What?
  - What is this theory about?
  - What is my understanding of it?
  - What do I need to ask in order to understand fully?
- So what?
  - So what might the implications of it be for me as a future police officer?
  - So what effects might it have for an individual's behaviour?
- Now what?
  - Now what situations could I apply this to?
  - Now what are my views on this theory?
  - Now what criticisms of the theory could I consider?

PRACTICAL TASK

In a future learning session, practise asking the above questions in your head as you are learning some new material.

Reflecting in a classroom situation

There may also be some occasions during your learning in which you wish to make an assessment of a situation while it is taking place. An example of this may be a presentation that you have been asked to make, or an academic debate that you feel is becoming confrontational. It may be that you feel uncomfortable about the way that the situation is progressing and wish to change your approach very quickly. In these types of situations Borton's model may be used to reflect in action. This allows you to make an assessment of the event while it is taking place and think consciously about the most appropriate response to it, rather than simply acting on instinct. Consider the following example of an event that may take place in the classroom.

You are discussing the topic of domestic violence in a small group and make a particular comment about your views. One of the other students in your group appears to have become upset and states that they are very sensitive about this issue. You therefore fear that the discussion may be distressing them.

Here, we break down the process that may be taking place in your mind as the situation progresses.

- What?
  - What is happening?
  - What is my involvement?
  - What could happen?
- So what?
  - So what are the implications of this?
  - So what might the effects of this be?
- Now what?
  - Now what could I do to improve the situation?
  - Now what might the consequences be?

PRACTICAL TASK

In a future learning situation, practise asking yourself the above questions while a situation is taking place.

Reflecting in practice

A final use for Borton's model for reflecting in action is to assist with making rapid practice decisions. This is similar to the type of reflection in action described in the classroom example above. You will undoubtedly become confident and experienced in dealing with a huge range of different situations during your future career as a police officer. It is therefore likely that, as Jasper (2003) suggests, your response to these situations may often be automatic and instinctive. There may be some occasions, however, where you wish to make a conscious decision about your actions. This may be in response to a situation that feels very unfamiliar or a situation that could be potentially dangerous, for example. Borton's model can be used in order to assess a situation very quickly, and it may therefore be used to assist you in thinking consciously about the task that you are undertaking as part of your everyday practice, rather than simply responding instinctively.

We can consider any future situation that you may be involved in as a police officer; this may include liaising with a member of the community or handling an emergency situation, for example. The types of question that you may ask yourself are listed below.

- What?
  - What is happening?
  - What is changing about this situation?
  - What are my actions?
- So what?
  - What are the implications?
  - What could happen if I act?
  - What could happen if I don't?
- Now what?
  - What should I do?
  - Is there anything more I need to know?
  - What might the consequences of my preferred actions be?

Reflecting on action
Here, we consider some of the ways in which Borton's model can be used in order to reflect on action.

Relating academic theory to practice
As a future police officer who has graduated from an academic programme, you will have gained the kinds of underpinning knowledge that assist you in understanding the social contexts in which particular events take place. As considered in Chapter 1, this is an important development in policing because the theoretical material that you have gained is intended to assist in making sense of complicated situations in the future, and therefore in making competent practice decisions. Some examples of how reflection may be used in order to relate theory to practice are considered in the next chapter.

Learning how to learn: developing your practice skills
As you progress through your career you will encounter a huge variety of different situations; indeed, it is unlikely that two days will be the same. There will be some situations in which you feel that you performed well, and others in which you feel you could have performed more effectively. Reflecting regularly will assist you in thinking continually of ways that you can improve in order to strengthen your skills for effective practice. This can be thought of as relating old practice to new practice.

PRACTICAL TASK

Consider this example of a future policing situation.

You are attending a meeting with a local community group. You are aware that confidence in the police is a particular problem in this area, and your local police force is attempting to address this. A member of the group becomes hostile towards you and you are unable to defuse the situation. Reinforcements are therefore called upon.

Now consider the following questions.

- *What?*
  - *What happened during the event?*
  - *What actions did I take?*
  - *What was the result of these actions?*
- *So what?*
  - *So what influence did my actions have upon the outcome?*
  - *So what might have happened if I had not reacted in this way?*
  - *So what might I consider doing differently next time?*
- *Now what?*
  - *Now what do I need to learn in order to improve my performance?*
  - *Now what approaches would I take in a similar situation?*
  - *Now what might the consequences of these approaches be?*

It is important to note there will inevitably be some situations for which you feel that you have limited practice knowledge or training. The reflective model can be used to identify the gaps in your knowledge and the actions that you can take in order to correct this. Similarly, you may also reflect upon any advice that you have been offered in order to assess how this advice has improved your ability to address similar situations. The types of question that could be asked are: What advice was I given? So what effect did this have? Now what will I do next time?

Driscoll's model of reflection (2000)

A further model of reflection is an adaptation of Borton's developmental framework presented by Driscoll. He refers to this as the What? model of structured reflection (2000, p27). Each of the questions 'What?' 'So what?' and 'Now what?' that Borton refers to are asked again, but much more detail is provided in relation to each of the sections. Driscoll suggests that the model can be adapted to the needs of the reflector and should therefore be regarded as a prompt or trigger, rather than 'a right way to reflect' (Driscoll, 2000, p27). Borton's model is very useful for students who are new to reflective practice. It is also flexible in the ways that it can be applied. While it is therefore recommended for you as a police student to use, you may feel that you are already confident enough as a reflector to consider a more thorough level of reflective analysis. Driscoll's model may therefore be useful for some of your reflections, and it is outlined here.

What?

The 'What?' element of the model asks you to consider the following types of question (Driscoll, 2000, p28).

- What is the reason for thinking about this situation?
- What exactly took place?
- What did you see?
- What did you do?
- What was your reaction?
- What did others do?
- What do you think was the key aspect in this situation?

So what?

The following types of question may be asked (Driscoll, 2000, p28).

- What were your feelings at the time?
- What are your feelings now and how might they differ?
- What effects did your actions have?
- What good emerged from the situation?
- What troubles you about it?
- What were your feelings in comparison to your colleagues?
- What are the reasons for feeling differently from your colleagues?

Now what?

Finally, Driscoll (2000, p28) suggests the following types of question.

- What needs to happen to change the situation?
- What are the implications and consequences for you?
- What are you going to do about the situation?
- What happens if you decide not to do anything?
- What might you do differently if faced with a similar situation again?
- What information do you need in order to face a similar situation again?

REFLECTIVE TASK

Consider a situation that has happened to you recently. Write down your reflections using Driscoll's model as a guide.

Gibbs's reflective cycle

As previously discussed, professionals such as nurses, social workers and teachers have been required to practise in a reflective way for many years. In order to assist with this activity, a series of reflective models have been developed. Perhaps one of the most influential of these was devised within the nursing profession by Gibbs (1988).

Jasper (2003) suggests that Gibbs's reflective cycle was inspired by the experiential learning cycle presented by Kolb (1984) and described in Chapter 2. Gibbs's cycle includes seven stages in which a series of questions are answered. Although this may feel like a long-winded process at first, one of the main strengths of this model is that it allows the reflector to make a very detailed assessment of everything that happened during a particular event. Rather than simply concluding that a situation was good or bad overall, it can take into consideration the fact that most situations are complicated, and that some elements of them will probably have been more successful than others. By using a detailed model, it is therefore possible to consider many different aspect of a situation, and to ask questions such as: What worked well for me? What could I improve for future situations? Were there any circumstances that I could not control? What skills could I develop in order to address a similar situation more effectively?

Another important advantage of this model is that it asks the individual to reflect upon the feelings that they had during the event. Talking about our emotions is not always something that is encouraged during our professional lives. Moon (1999) suggests that this is a result of Western culture in which an emphasis is placed upon logic and problem solving. As considered in the last chapter, however, it is often the case that our instincts and emotions influence the practical decisions that we make, particularly when we are faced with situations that require us to form an impression very quickly. Reflecting back upon the feelings that we experienced during an event can help to identify the things that motivated our behaviour at the time. We will consider Gibbs's model of reflection in more detail (Gibbs, 1988, p41).

Stage 1: Describing the event
The first stage of the cycle is to think back to a particular event and consider everything that happened. You may wish to do this by describing it to someone else, by thinking about it privately or by writing it down. Try to consider as many things about the event as you can remember so that your memory of it is as clear as possible. At this stage it is important to avoid reaching a conclusion about the event; it should simply be described.

Stage 2: Exploring your feelings
The second element of the cycle asks you to consider your thoughts, feelings and emotions during the event. These are often the things that influence our actions at an

instinctive or sometimes consious level. It is sometimes difficult to talk about our emotions within the professional context, and this stage of the cycle is therefore a useful opportunity to reflect upon them privately. You may wish to consider how others made you feel during the event, and whether your feelings changed during the event.

Stage 3: Evaluating the event

The evaluation element of the cycle allows you to form an impression of the situation as a whole and measure its importance or value. Often this can be done by comparing it to other experiences that you have had in order to assess the similarities and differences. There are two basic questions that may be asked.

- What were the positive elements of the experience?

- Were there any negative elements?

These questions can also be put in the following way.

- What went well?

- What did not work so well?

Stage 4: Analysis of the event

The previous stage asked you to consider your overall impressions of the event. The analysis part of the cycle asks you to think about everything that happened in detail, and to formulate an opinion about it. By doing this you can consider the situation from various different angles in order to make sense of it (Jasper, 2003). You may consider the things that you did well, the elements of the situation that were good, and the reasons why you decided upon the particular actions taken.

Stage 5: Forming a general conclusion

Here, you are asked to consider your overall assessment of the situation and the general conclusion that you have reached.

Stage 6: Forming a specific conclusion

Because you have analysed the situation in detail, you should now be able to draw some conclusions about your own performance. There may be particular elements of the situation that you could not possibly have predicted or you could not have had any control over. For other parts of the event you may have been happy with the things that you did, or you may feel that you could have behaved differently. You can start to formulate some conclusions about what you could do in the future if a similar situation arose. This stage of the cycle is also useful for helping you to assess your own specific strengths and weaknesses in particular situations, and any skills that you may wish to develop and improve. Consider asking yourself the following questions.

- What elements of my performance was I happy with?

- Is there anything that I would do again in a similar situation?

- Can I identify any particular strengths or skills that I already have?

- Is there anything that I could have done differently?

- Are there any situations I am not as good at dealing with?

- What skills could I improve?

Stage 7: Making a personal action plan

The final stage of the cycle is important because it asks you to make some concrete plans for how you will perform differently or perhaps similarly in future situations. At this point the process of converting thoughts into actions begins. You can therefore start to take a practical approach to your continued development and improvement.

Some examples of the specific types of question that you may ask in order to plan future actions are as follows.

- What will I repeat if a similar situation occurs?

- What things will I approach differently?

- What actions can I take in order to improve my skills?

- Is there anything more that I need to know in order to perform effectively in the future?

REFLECTIVE TASK

1 *Think back to a situation or event that has taken place recently. This may be something that happened in the classroom during your studies, or in a work-based environment if you are engaged in any employment at the moment. If it is difficult for you to recall an example that you could use, you may consider something that has happened recently within your private life.*

2 *Follow the description of each stage of Gibbs's reflective cycle outlined above and answer as many of the questions about the event as you can.*

3 *For the final stage of the cycle, complete the following three sentences in order to plan your future actions.*

If I am in a similar situation in the future . . .

1 Next time I would repeat . . .

2 Next time I would not . . .

3 A skill I could develop is . . .

Now reflect upon the situation again using Borton's (1970) model and Driscoll's (2000) model. Consider which of these you prefer. You may decide that you would like to use all of these models but vary them according to the type of situation. Borton's model, for example, may be more suitable for you when reflecting in action, but you may choose to use Gibbs's model when reflecting after an event. We consider some methods for structuring your reflective time in Chapter 6.

Reflective skills assessment

Consider again the questions that you asked yourself at the start of the chapter. Compare your answers in order to assess your learning.

1 How reflective am I as a learner?

2 When could I reflect 'on' my actions?

3 Are there any occasions when I could reflect 'in' action?

4 What models of reflection have I heard of?

C H A P T E R   S U M M A R Y

This chapter has introduced a selection of practical tools in order to assist you in starting to become a reflective learner. First, it considered some of the principles of reflection. The chapter then introduced a very simple model of reflection referred to as Borton's developmental framework (1970). A variety of uses for this model were described. A second model by Driscoll (2000) was introduced, which expands upon Borton's work. Finally, Gibbs's (1988) model of reflection was described. You should now have a better idea of some of the frameworks that can be used in order to assist you in starting to become a reflective learner.

FURTHER READING

A fuller understanding of Gibbs's model and approach to adult learning can be obtained from Gibbs (1988) *Learning by doing: a guide to teaching and learning methods.* The full reference is listed below.

REFERENCES

Borton, T (1970) *Reach, touch and teach.* New York: Mcgraw-Hill.

Driscoll, J (2000) *Practising clinical supervision.* Edinburgh: Ballierre Tindall.

Gibbs, G (1988) *Learning by doing: a guide to teaching and learning methods.* Oxford: Oxford Polytechnic.

Jasper, M (2003) *Beginning reflective practice.* London: Nelson Thornes.

Jasper, M (2006) *Professional development, reflection and decision-making.* Oxford: Blackwell Publishing.

Johns, C (2009) *Becoming a reflective practitioner.* Chichester: Wiley-Blackwell.

Kolb, D A (1984) *Experiential learning: experience as a source of learning and development.* Upper Saddle River NJ: Prentice Hall.

Moon, J (1999) *Reflection in learning and professional development*. Oxford: RoutledgeFalmer.

Schön, D (1983) *The reflective practitioner*. San Francisco CA: Jossey-Bass.

USEFUL WEBSITES

www.heacademy.ac.uk/ourwork/teachingandlearning/pdp

www.heacademy.ac.uk/assets/hlst/documents/resource_guides/foundation_degree_students_in_reflective_learning.pdf

The Higher Education Academy provides details of the development and use of PDP for Students in Higher Education.

5 The first steps: relating theory to practice

CHAPTER OBJECTIVES

By the end of this chapter you will have:

- explored some of the challenges of modern policing;
- understood why it is necessary to apply theory to practice;
- reflected upon a selection of policing case scenarios;
- practised applying a range of theories from your learning to your understanding of practical policing situations.

LINKS TO STANDARDS

This chapter provides opportunities for links with the following Skills for Justice, National Occupational Standards (NOS) for Policing and Law Enforcement 2008.

AE1   Maintain and develop your own knowledge, skills and competence.
CD1   Provide an initial response to incidents.
GC10   Manage conflict.
AA1   Promote equality and value diversity.
AB1   Communicate effectively with people.

Introduction

This chapter provides you with an opportunity to begin using your reflective skills in order to relate theory to practice. It starts by considering the complexity of modern policing and the reasons why reflective skills are necessary. The requirement that police officers understand the communities that they serve and inspire public confidence is considered. The chapter then provides a range of case scenarios. You will be invited to use Borton's reflective model in order to consider how some of the theories that you have learned throughout your studies may inform your understanding of practical policing situations in the future. Three areas will be considered: neighbourhood policing and community issues;

equality and diversity; and the needs of victims of crime. The key feature of this chapter is that it demonstrates the importance of developing thinking skills for day-to-day police practice.

The primary focus of this chapter is the use of reflection 'on' action. This is so that you may consider how some of the theories that you have learned during your studies can be applied to your understanding of real-life policing situations in the future. We start with a knowledge check – a series of questions designed to assess your current understanding of how your academic learning may aid your future policing practice. You will be invited to revisit these questions at the end of the chapter so that you can assess your learning.

REFLECTIVE TASK

Knowledge check

Write down your answers to the following questions.

- *What do I know about modern policing?*

- *What types of knowledge and theory have I learned during my studies?*

- *Why are these theories important for policing?*

Relating theory to policing practice

Previous chapters have introduced you to the importance of reflection for adult learning. Now that you have had the opportunity to start practising your reflective skills, we begin to place them in the context of modern policing in order to explore the ways that reflection may assist you in applying your theoretical knowledge to practical situations. It is useful to start by considering the varied and complex role of the modern police officer and the reasons why being a reflective, knowledgeable practitioner are considered necessary.

The modern police officer

Throughout your studies you will have been introduced to the broad range of tasks that police officers undertake during the course of their duties. There is no doubt that law enforcement is a key responsibility for the police, and it may be that this is one of the main reasons for choosing to pursue a future career as a police officer. Many commentators have suggested that policing is not restricted simply to fighting crime but involves a whole range of activities that are often community rather than crime related.

Think about any encounters that you or someone you know has experienced with the police service. Write down your answers to the following questions.

1 How many of these situations involved a criminal offence?

2 What other types of event have involved the police?

3 What types of activity were the police engaged in?

The range of policing activities

Coleman and Norris (2000, p122) describe a range of activities that police officers may undertake during the course of their duties. Some are listed here.

- Searching for a lost child.

- Settling a dispute between two neighbours about a parking space.

- Attending a sudden death.

- Securing entry to a house in order to check the safety of an elderly relative.

- Informing a local resident of the death of a relative.

- Dispersing a crowd of young people who are congregating on a street corner.

- Helping a bus driver remove a disruptive passenger.

- Attending a neighbourhood watch meeting.

- Taking a report at the scene of a burglary at which the home owner was absent.

These examples demonstrate only a small number of the situations that the police face, and many of them have little or no direct relationship to crime or law enforcement. Waddington and Wright (2010) suggest that at the heart of policing is the need to intervene in situations that members of the public feel unable to control themselves. The role of the police officer is therefore diverse, and requires a range of skills and knowledge in order to adapt quickly to a multitude of situations.

While the role of the police officer is not the main focus of this book, in this chapter it is important to consider the link between reflective skills and policing work. This is because the underpinning knowledge that you will no doubt develop throughout the course of your studies, combined with the ability to be reflective, will assist you in making sense of very complicated social situations in the future. This will allow you not only to adapt quickly to a variety of different events but also to make competent practice decisions based upon your understanding of *why* a particular course of action may be the most appropriate.

Consider an example from the list of police activities given above, provided by Coleman and Norris (2000). Jot down some of the theories that you have been introduced to during your studies. Think about whether any of these could be used to help you understand and respond to your chosen situation. Here we use Borton's (1970) reflective model as a guide. An example is provided to help you start.

Attending the scene of a sudden death

- *What?*

  - *What theories might help me understand this situation?*

  - *What are the effects of grief?*

  - *What about culture?*

  - *What about gender?*

- *So what?*

  - *So what do I know about the ways that people behave when they have suffered a bereavement?*

  - *So what cultural issues might need to be considered, depending upon the religion of the person that has died?*

  - *So what are the gender differences in the way that women and men may respond to the death of a relative (if any)?*

- *Now what?*

  - *Now what could I do in order to help a grieving relative?*

  - *Now what special cultural or religious arrangements might need to be made for the person that has died?*

  - *Now what type of interpersonal skills might I need to use while assisting different members of the public?*

Using the example above to help you, consider your answers to the What? So what? Now what? questions.

The need to improve public confidence

Not only is policing a diverse role but it is one that is constantly evolving and changing. We saw in Chapter 1 that the training and education that student police officers receive have been radically transformed since the publication of *Training matters* (Home Office, 2002), the first inspection of the initial police training programme. This was largely in response to the changing nature of policing and the desire for a learning programme that reflected the needs of a modernised service. A key component of this was the recognition that public confidence in the police needed to improve.

Here, we briefly consider some of the historical events that have influenced the development of the modern police service and contributed to the need for police officers who are socially knowledgeable and reflective. A fuller understanding of the role of the police can be obtained by reading *What is policing?* (Waddington and Wright, 2010). The full reference for this book and similar texts are listed at the end of the chapter.

PRACTICAL TASK

Watch any fictional British television programme that describes the culture and practice of the police in the 1970s or 1980s. It may be useful to consider an episode of Life on Mars, Ashes to Ashes or The Sweeney. If you are unable to access a full episode of this type of programme, it may be possible to view a short section from a website such as YouTube. As you watch the programme, make some notes in relation to the following.

1 The language used to describe the following groups.

- *Offenders or suspects.*

- *Women.*

- *Individuals from black and minority ethnic backgrounds.*

2 The general manner and style used when communicating with the public.

3 The types of task that the police characters engaged in.

Assuming that this is an accurate representation of the attitudes and behaviour of the police during this period, consider the following questions.

1 How might the police have viewed the public?

2 How might the public have viewed the police?

3 To what extent did the police engage with communities?

4 Are there any particular social groups that may have found it difficult to engage with or trust the police?

Historical tensions

Many criminologists and social theorists have commented upon the historical tensions between the public and the police. Crawford (1998), for example, refers to a series of social incidents and miscarriages of justice during the 1970s and 1980s that resulted in a growing sense of injustice regarding police behaviour. The Brixton riots in London and the Toxteth riots in Liverpool, both in 1981, resulted in large numbers of public and police casualties. The riots were brought about by a combination of social factors, including high levels of unemployment and poverty in inner-city areas, and a dissatisfaction with the ways that some members of the police force behaved towards minority ethnic groups. What followed, largely as a result of the Brixton riots, was a report by Lord Scarman (1981). Lord Scarman concluded that the public's confidence in the police had to a large extent been lost. Police forces, he suggested, should seek to find better ways of engaging with the community. This can be considered in keeping with the original vision of Robert Peel, the founder of the modern police force. In this, the 'bobby on the beat' was a visible presence who worked closely with the community. As we shall see, this belief re-emerged as the basis for what was much later to become community policing.

The police and victims of crime

Mawby (2007) suggests that there are three key reasons why the police should be mindful of the needs of victims.

- The police rely upon victims to report crime.

- The police are the main agency dealing with the victims of crime.

- Historically, the police have a poor record when supporting the victims of crime, especially victims of rape and domestic violence.

Institutional racism

A series of incidents since the 1990s also appeared to confirm the suspicion that the police force did not fully understand or cater for the needs of a diverse society. As we saw in Chapter 1, the police mismanagement of the Stephen Lawrence murder brought the issue of institutional racism in some areas of the police service to the attention of the government and the public, despite the recommendations of the Scarman Report several years earlier. A more detailed understanding of the importance of the Scarman Report, the Stephen Lawrence Inquiry and broader equality and diversity issues can be obtained by referring to *Equality and diversity in policing* (Stout, 2010), another title in this series. The full reference for this text is provided at the end of the chapter.

Reiner (2010) also refers to two examples of undercover journalism that highlighted similar issues. *The secret policeman* (2003) was a documentary in which a reporter secretly joined the police force. Several incidents of institutional and overt racism were identified. *The undercover copper* (2006) followed and identified similar problems, this time in relation to sexist attitudes displayed by individual police officers.

The desire to restore confidence

It is possible to see from the history of community relationships with the public why public confidence is such an important issue for modern policing. Rix et al. (2009) suggest in their government research report that public confidence is now the single most important policing priority. They also identify four key areas that are effective in restoring the public's faith in the police. These are listed below.

- Community policing – including officers engaged with the public on foot patrol, identifying local priorities with their community through consultation and problem solving.

- Good quality community engagement – involving contact with local residents while based within the community, and responding to requests for help from the public in a respectful and polite way.

- Local communication by newsletter – including clear information about local services, community priorities and planned courses of action.

- Restorative justice – involving a process in which the victim and the offender are brought together in order to seek a resolution of their conflict.

PRACTICAL TASK

Visit the Customer Care Guide at the National Police Improvement Agency website. This can be found at the following web address.

www.npia.police.uk/en/docs/NPIA_customer_guide.pdf

Write a list of the things contained within it that may assist in improving public confidence.

For the reasons highlighted, community policing is now regarded as the most effective form of policing. It is to this that we now briefly turn.

A modern service – community policing

The principles of community policing are far from new; in fact, they are at the heart of what Robert Peel intended the police officer to be – a responsive member of the public who understands the community that they serve, and works closely within it in order to maintain public order. As we saw earlier, this was identified as one of the solutions to public dissatisfaction by Lord Scarman as long ago as 1981. Reiner and Newburn (2007) suggest that community policing emerged not only from the recognition that public confidence had deteriorated but also from the specific desire to engage with what are often referred to as 'hard to reach' groups. These are particular communities that may include black and minority ethnic groups, travellers and the gay community, for example. Traditionally these groups may have been suspicious of the police service.

Reiner and Newburn (2007) further suggest that there is not a particular model or template for community policing; rather, the policing styles and tactics employed should be appropriate to the specific needs of the particular community. These may be very different for a rural area of North Yorkshire and a multicultural inner-city area. The consistent theme is that the approach is based upon an understanding of the diverse needs of particular community groups, and is locally agreed upon.

PRACTICAL TASK

If you are able to, contact a police officer via the website Twitter and ask them about their role. The website address is **http://twitter.com/policelists/uk-police-on-twitter**.

You may wish to ask what the local priorities are and if there are any particular social issues that relate to their particular community.

Improving confidence – the importance of reflection

We now return to the main focus of this book, which is reflective practice. The developments in policing outlined above will require you to be a very different type of officer than you might have been during the 1970s or 1980s, for example. Although it is still the case that police officers respond to crime and deal with emergency situations, the emphasis is placed upon proactive, preventative policing rather than simply reacting to the consequences of crime after it has taken place. Policing is therefore as complex as it has ever been, if not more so. It requires an understanding of diversity and community issues and the needs of the victims of crime. It is very likely that this is the type of learning that you are engaged in during your current studies.

One of the reasons why reflective skills are an essential tool for a future police officer is that they enable you to apply your theoretical knowledge to real-world situations. The difference here is that instead of simply being trained to react to situations, modern police officers are also educated in order that they may learn to think independently. They are therefore able to make informed judgements based upon their reflective skills. We consider the importance of judgement and discretion in the next section of this chapter.

Inspiring confidence – a personal responsibility

The ability to gain the confidence of the public can be regarded as both a service-wide and a personal responsibility. While the structures for community policing are now firmly embedded, the ability to form good relationships with your community in the future will be largely dependent upon your use of police discretion and the general manner and style in which you present yourself as a professional. Waddington and Wright (2010) point out the very public nature of policing work. They suggest that, regardless of the mode of transport, be it car, bicycle or on foot, the streets are the stage on which the police officer performs. The performance is therefore one in which the mere presence of the officer provides reassurance to the public.

Although we focus upon the ability to make reflective practical decisions in the latter section of this chapter, it is useful to start by considering the interpersonal skills that you bring to your future policing role (and, indeed, to your current learning). These are the skills and abilities that you already possess in communicating effectively with others. Many of these will have been developed throughout your life and during your current studies, and can therefore be regarded as transferable skills. In Chapter 2 we considered how these can be identified using reflection. We explore these in further detail in the final chapter of the book when examining your skills for employability. Here, we use Borton's model in order to assess the communication skills that you already have and those that you may need to develop in order to build trusting relationships with the public in the future.

REFLECTIVE TASK

Think about the skills that you possess as an effective communicator. It may be useful to consider a range of situations that you have previously been involved in. These may have included comforting a distressed relative or explaining a task to a small child, for example. Using Borton's model, answer the following questions.

- *What?*
  - *What are my strengths as a communicator and do they relate to written or verbal communication?*
  - *What particular situations am I good at dealing with?*
  - *What roles and situations did I learn these skills from?*
- *So what?*
  - *So what situations might my skills be useful for in my role as a police officer?*
  - *So what might the benefits be of having these skills?*
- *Now what?*
  - *Now what can I do to enhance and maintain these skills?*

This exercise is particularly useful because listing the strengths and abilities that you have will also help you identify the deficits – or gaps – in your communication skills. Consider the reflective cycle again, and this time list the skills that you would like to improve.

- *What?*
  - *What situations am I not as effective in dealing with as a communicator?*
  - *What skills would I like to improve?*
- *So what?*
  - *So what might the consequences of not possessing these skills be for me?*
  - *So what might the consequences be for others?*
- *Now what?*
  - *Now what skills would I like to strengthen and develop?*
  - *Now what can I do in order to develop these skills?*

Finally, having identified your strengths and weaknesses, write a short action plan containing the following two sections.

- *What can I do to maintain and improve the skills that I have?*
- *What can I do to develop the skills that I do not yet possess?*

Reflection and individual interpretation

A final point regarding the role of the modern police officer is the use of reflection for the interpretation of events. Within the policing role, as with most others, there are few situations that are entirely straightforward. Most events will require the police officer to form a judgement and act accordingly. Although there are undoubtedly situations in which an offence has clearly taken place, Coleman and Norris (2000) suggest that even the decision to make an arrest carries with it a degree of discretionary power.

REFLECTIVE TASK

Consider the following situation.

Coleman and Norris (2000) provide an example of two men who are fighting on a street corner. When the police arrive the men are still fighting. List the possible courses of action that you think could be taken.

Coleman and Norris suggest that there are, in fact, five ways that this situation may be resolved. These are listed below.

1 Stop the men from fighting and take no further action.

2 After breaking up the fight, find out the causes of it and help the men resolve them.

3 Caution one or both men.

4 Attempt to find out who has caused the fight and make an arrest.

5 Arrest both men.

Here we see that even in a relatively simple situation there are a number of legitimate actions that could be taken. In fact, any one of these responses could be the right answer. A police officer will therefore need to use reflective skills in order to arrive at an appropriate response. This becomes even more significant when we consider the increasingly diverse role of the modern police officer. In the future, you may often be formulating your own theory as to what the problem is and what the intervention should be. It therefore becomes vital to be able to make thoughtful, educated decisions based upon your understanding of what motivates particular behaviours. It is the ability to use reflective practice in order to link theory to practice that we now turn. We considered the additional role that our values and beliefs play in decision making in Chapter 3.

Some practical examples

Some practical examples of possible policing situations are provided so that you can begin to reflect upon some of the theories that you have learned during your studies, and consider how they may help you to understand practical and sometimes very complicated situations. The areas for consideration have been designed to fit with the priorities of modern policing, so examples relating to community policing, equality and diversity issues, and the needs of victims of crime will be considered. Borton's reflective model is again used as a guide. We start by considering a diversity and community issue.

Diversity and equality example

CASE STUDY

A police officer visited a school in order to provide a teaching session for a group of children. Suddenly she was called to the playground where two boys appeared to be fighting. As she approached she saw that both of the boys were Asian and approximately ten years old. One boy had fallen to the ground and the other was about to hit him. A crowd of children had gathered.

REFLECTIVE TASK

Consider the following questions according to Borton's model.

What?

- *What do you think may have been happening here?*
- *What else might the real cause of this problem have been?*
- *What theories have you learned that might help you understand what was happening?*

The immediate reaction to this situation would usually be simply to stop the boys from fighting. By doing this the situation may be easily resolved. Although the prevention of harm is the upmost priority, it is also important to understand some of the factors that may have caused this situation. These may be far less obvious. Consider some of your recent learning. You may have an awareness of some of the factors that motivate aggression or bullying, for example, but what about the ethnicity of the boys? Have you also considered their ages or their backgrounds? Far from being a simple situation, these factors may lead you to believe that there was something much more complicated taking place.

REFLECTIVE TASK

So what?

- *So what might these issues mean when explaining the situation?*
- *So what were the options for dealing with this situation?*
- *So what might have happened if the situation had not been resolved?*

Here we start to apply our knowledge so that the situation makes sense. It therefore becomes more than simply a procedural issue – 'the boys were fighting so we needed to split them up'. Instead, we understand why they were fighting and what the underlying problem was. This way, we can think about resolving the problem and, most importantly, prevent it from occurring in the future.

REFLECTIVE TASK

Now what?

- *Now what can be done to resolve this situation?*

Here, we may be able to think creatively about a solution to this problem. The strategy employed may not have been identified without the background knowledge that you have considered. This example demonstrates that reflection can be used to understand situations and respond to them in a thoughtful way, rather than simply reacting to what is seen.

The following case study expands upon the exercise above. It describes a real-life example of a similar situation that involved a newly qualified police officer who had also undertaken a police studies course.

CASE STUDY

Sarah had been a qualified police officer for six months when she started working at a local school. This was as part of a 'Safer Schools Project', an initiative designed to engage hard-to-reach groups with the police and ensure that children attended their local school. Sarah intervened in the fight between the two boys and spoke to both of them about the incident. She discovered that the fight itself was a relatively minor incident; however, it was a symptom of a much larger problem. Both of the boys were Muslim, one from a Sunni community, and the other from a Shia community. Tension between these groups had been slowly building within the school, but this had gone unnoticed.

Sarah knew from both her studies and her experience that there had been a history of difficult relationships between these particular groups in her community. She was also aware that young people are often difficult to reach by the police, and are more likely to be dealt with as offenders rather than victims of crime. She therefore felt that her choice of action was important because it could prevent the tensions from escalating further. She also wished to resolve the situation as informally as possible so that the boys were not introduced to the criminal justice system unnecessarily.

Sarah reflected upon the situation and found a creative solution. She liaised with the headteacher, and a meeting between parents, teachers, community leaders and the local policing team was called in order to assist the community in identifying solutions to this

---

CASE STUDY *continued*

problem. The group decided to apply for some local funding, which had been made available from the Proceeds of Crime Fund in the local area. Children from both communities were invited to attend a supervised fishing trip together. During this excursion the children were encouraged to learn more about each other and to develop friendly relationships.

This process can be summarised as follows.

What?

A fight had broken out in the playground; however the real problem related to cultural tensions within the school.

So what?

Sarah's knowledge about cultural issues informed her of the potential for community relationships to deteriorate, and for the boys involved to be punished unnecessarily. This might have damaged relationships between the police and young people within the area, and Sarah was keen to avoid this. It was therefore considered important to intervene in a positive and constructive way.

Now what?

A creative solution was decided upon by the community, which aimed to repair community relationships.

Community policing example

We consider a further example of a community issue. You are invited to start to consider some of the theories that you may have learned about the possible causes of crime. By reflecting upon them, it may be possible to identify some solutions to the social problems that are identified.

CASE STUDY

In a busy inner-city area the local police force identified that there had been an increase in the number of reported burglaries. Unemployment within the area was higher than the national average. A number of the housing estates had deteriorated in condition and drug-related incidents had increased.

> ### REFLECTIVE TASK
>
> *Consider a police officer working within a community policing team. How might they have assisted the community in reducing the number of burglaries and drug offences?*
>
> *What?*
>
> - *What do you think the main issues were?*
>
> - *What theories do you think could be applied in order to understand the increased level of crime in this area?*

Think carefully about the main social issues. What do you think the effects of unemployment may have been, for example? Are there any other potential causes of the problems? Then think about any theories about the causes of crime that you may know. An example to help you start is social exclusion – what do you think this may be?

> ### REFLECTIVE TASK
>
> *So what?*
>
> - *So what action could the officer have taken?*
>
> - *So what might the benefits or consequences of these actions be?*

By reflecting upon the things that may have caused the increase in burglaries and drug offences, it is possible to start to consider some solutions. You may consider the social and criminological theories that you have applied. Again, it might have been possible simply to react to offences after they have taken place – policing the area and making arrests. Although there is no doubt that the police do respond to crime, it is important to consider whether this alone could address the underlying causes. Are there any other proactive measures that could have been taken in order to help the community reduce their crime rate?

> ### REFLECTIVE TASK
>
> *Now what?*
>
> - *Now what might the most effective course of action be?*

Think about some of the things that the officer might have done in order to assist the community. Again, by using this reflective process, we see how an understanding of theory can be used in order to resolve problems rather than merely react to the consequences of them.

We can examine the above example in more detail. There are several issues that may have caused the increase in burglaries, and you may have identified some of these. You might have considered the levels of unemployment and potential poverty, for example. You may have thought about the influence of drug problems. There are also theories from criminology that could be applied. You may have been introduced to ideas such as social exclusion or 'broken windows' theory (Wilson and Kelling, 2005), for example. This promotes the policing of minor crimes in order to prevent more serious crimes occurring. You may consider how these theories could add to your understanding of the problems within the area.

Leaving these issues unresolved may result in the levels of crime continuing to rise. It may, indeed, be possible to respond to any further incidents by dealing with the consequences and not the causes, but this will not get to the heart of the problem. Here, we see why it is far more effective to understand the causes of crime and identify solutions that prevent it from occurring.

There are several things that the officer may have considered in order to help the community reduce the crime rate. For some real examples of the measures that the police take, you may wish to visit the website for your own police service where the range of crime prevention measures in your area will be outlined. In this example, the officer may have considered the following.

- Become a more visible presence within the areas. As we discussed earlier in the chapter, this may simply involve being the 'bobby on the beat' and providing reassurance to the local community.

- Building confidence with the community and developing trusting relationships. This may involve employing the types of interpersonal skills that you identified earlier.

- Working with individual members of the community in order to provide them with information about security, and helping them make their homes safer.

- Consulting with the community policing team, other social agencies and the community in order to identify solutions to problems such as unemployment and social exclusion.

Again, we may summarise the above example using Borton's reflective model.

What?
There was an increase in crime in the local area, including drug-related incidents and burglaries. Unemployment and poverty had contributed to the problem and some groups of individuals felt excluded from the wider community.

So what?
The problems may have escalated, resulting in more frequent arrests. Members of the community may have become increasingly socially excluded and resentful of the police.

Now what?
Having reflected upon the situation, the officer has applied his knowledge of some of the causes of crime. He has been able to use this in order to help him change his practice. He

has worked more closely with the community in order to prevent crime in the future, and has engaged the policing team and other agencies in addressing some of the social problems.

'Needs of the victim' example

We now consider a final example that may help you to practise the art of relating theory to practice. Earlier we discussed the emphasis placed upon meeting the needs of the victims of crime in modern policing, and it is to this that we now turn. What follows is an imaginary example of a community policing situation.

CASE STUDY

Tom was a community support officer. He had been called on several occasions to a 'nuisance caller' in his community. The caller was an elderly resident who claimed that there were trespassers in his garden. No evidence has been found to support this. The man lived alone and did not leave the house very often. According to police records he had been a victim of robbery in the past.

REFLECTIVE TASK

- *What do you think the real issues may have been? There are several things within the example that you may wish to consider. Do you think the age of the man may have been significant? Might the fact that he had been a victim of crime in the past be a factor?*

- *So what might Tom have done? Should he have warned the man not to waste police time, for example? Are there any other courses of action that he might have considered?*

- *Now what? From your understanding of the underlying issues, consider what the best solutions may have been.*

We can consider the above example in more detail.

CASE STUDY

Tom spoke to the resident and found out more about him. He discovered that the main problem was, in fact, the fear of crime. Tom was aware that this was a common concern within the community. He was also conscious that the man did not leave his home very often because of this. He learned from his studies that this could result in feelings of isolation and exclusion.

CASE STUDY *continued*

Tom therefore took the following action. He used his listening skills in order to understand the key problems. He reassured the man about the levels of crime in the area and assured him that he would receive a local newsletter. He also helped to secure the house and garden. Finally, he liaised with Age UK and social services, in order to address some of the underlying problems.

This example relates to an issue raised at the beginning of the chapter: that modern policing is concerned with much more than simply apprehending criminals. Your future policing role may often involve providing a service to the community by offering support, guidance and reassurance.

Finally, we may summarise this reflection.

What?
Several calls have been made to the police by an elderly resident. The real problem is an underlying fear of crime.

So what?
The community support officer recognised that the man is isolated from the community and wished to help him become more included.

Now what?
The solution involved reassuring the resident and helping him secure his home. Efforts were also made to help him become more engaged in the community.

REFLECTIVE TASK

Knowledge check review

Answer the following questions and compare your answers with the ones you gave to the same questions at the beginning of the chapter so that you may assess your learning.

- *What do I know about modern policing?*
- *What types of knowledge and theory have I learned during my studies?*
- *Why are these theories important for policing?*

CHAPTER SUMMARY

This chapter has considered the role of the modern police officer and the importance of improving public confidence. It has explored the reasons why underpinning knowledge is important for policing. The chapter then provided a range of exercises designed to allow you to practise relating theory to practice. You should now have a better understanding of how reflective practice can be used in order to help you make effective competent practice decisions in your future policing role.

FURTHER READING

Stout (2010) *Equality and diversity in policing* provides students with a detailed understanding of the importance of equality and diversity issues for modern policing.

Waddington and Wright (2010) in *What is policing?* introduce students to the range of roles and responsibilities undertaken by individuals who perform a policing role. This book describes the complexity of modern policing practice, and students may therefore gain a fuller understanding of why the ability to be reflective may also be valuable.

REFERENCES

Borton, T (1970) *Reach, touch and teach*. New York: Mcgraw-Hill.

Coleman, C and Norris, C (2000) *Introducing criminology*. Cullompton: Willan.

Crawford, A (1998) *Community safety and crime prevention*. London: Addison Wesley Longman.

Home Office (2002) *Training matters*. London: Home Office. Available online at http://webarchive. nationalarchives.gov.uk/+/http://www.homeoffice.gov.uk/hmic/training_matters.pdf (accessed 27 October 2010).

Mawby, R (2007) Public sector service and the victim of crime, in Walklate, S (ed) *Handbook of victims and victimology*. Cullompton: Willan.

Reiner, R (2010) *Politics of the police*, 4th edition. Oxford: Oxford University Press.

Reiner, R and Newburn, T (2007) *Oxford handbook of criminology*. Oxford: Oxford University Press.

Rix, A, Joshua, F, Maguire, M and Morton, S (2009) *Improving public confidence in the police: a review of the evidence*. London: Home Office. Available online at http://rds.homeoffice.gov.uk/ rds/pdfs09/horr28b.pdf (accessed 10 May 2010).

Scarman, Lord (1981) *The Brixton disorders 12–14 April 1981: report of an inquiry by the Rt Hon Lord Scarman OBE*. London: HMSO.

Stout, B (2010) *Equality and diversity in policing*. Exeter: Learning Matters.

Waddington, P and Wright, M (2010) *What is policing?* Exeter: Learning Matters.

Wilson, J and Kelling, G (2005) Broken windows: the police and neighbourhood safety, in Newburn, T (ed) *Handbook of policing*. Cullompton: Willan.

USEFUL WEBSITES

http://cfnp.npia.police.uk (National Policing Improvement Agency)

www.homeoffice.gov.uk/police/ (the police section of the Home Office website)

6 Strategies for enhancing reflection

CHAPTER OBJECTIVES

By the end of this chapter you will have:

- considered the uses of reflective practice;
- identified your personal learning style;
- explored a range of methods for strengthening your reflective abilities.

LINKS TO STANDARDS

This chapter provides opportunities for links with the following Skills for Justice, National Occupational Standards (NOS) for Policing and Law Enforcement 2008.

AE1   Maintain and develop your own knowledge, skills and competence.

Introduction

This chapter provides a range of methods and techniques that may assist you in becoming an effective reflective learner. It begins by providing a summary of the benefits of reflective activity identified in previous chapters. The chapter then considers the four types of adult learner as identified by Kolb (1984) and invites you to identify your own preferred learning style. Finally, a range of strategies and techniques is provided, which are designed to assist you in strengthening your reflective learning style and your reflective abilities as an adult lifelong learner. It is useful to start with a knowledge check in order to assess your current knowledge of how you may enhance your ability to reflect. You will be invited to revisit these questions at the end of the chapter in order to measure your learning.

PRACTICAL TASK

Knowledge check

Answer the following questions.

- *What are the uses of reflection within adult learning?*
- *To what extent do I consciously use reflective practice in order to enhance my learning?*
- *What strategies could I consider for strengthening my ability to reflect?*

Reflection as a state of mind

Previous chapters have considered not only the role that reflection plays in adult learning but also the variety of ways that it can be used consciously in order to enhance your development. So far, a range of reflective models have been introduced in order to help you start using reflection in a very practical way. While there is no doubt that models such as 'What? So what? Now what?' (Borton, 1970) are widely used as a guide, reflective practice should be more than simply a technique or just one element of your current learning curriculum. Rather, reflective thinking should be regarded as a way of continually making new discoveries about the world and therefore as a way of life rather than a series of isolated activities. Bolton refers to reflection as 'a state of mind' (2010, p3).

This chapter expands upon your knowledge of reflective activity and considers some strategies and techniques that can be used in order to strengthen your reflective abilities as a person. Kolb (1984) suggests that adult learners have a tendency towards one of four different learning styles and that only one of these is reflective by nature. The ability to think in a reflective way is therefore reasonably natural to some individuals. For others, however, it is an art form that requires development and a greater amount of practice. You are invited to identify your preferred learning style in the next section of this chapter.

A comparison between muscle training and mind training may be made here. It is usually regarded as common knowledge that physical exercise improves muscle strength and stamina; you may already visit the gymnasium or take part in a team sport, for example. Although it may seem like a strange idea at first, the brain can also be thought of as similar to a muscle that can be trained to be stronger. Because reflection is a type of thinking, it is therefore a mental process that strengthens over a period of time through practice. In other words, it is possible to train the mind to be more reflective and therefore train the mind to learn. Before exploring some of the techniques for strengthening your reflective abilities it is useful to revisit the various advantages of reflective practice. By doing this it is possible see why making time to improve your reflective style is a good investment for your current studies and your future career.

Think about your learning throughout previous chapters. Write down from memory the various uses of reflection that have already been considered.

Uses of reflective activity

Below is a summary of the ways that reflection can be used by an adult learner.

- As a mechanism for learning from past experience during your current studies (relating practice to theory).

- As a similar tool for learning during future educational events throughout your career.

- As a means of relating theoretical knowledge to practice situations as a future police officer.

- As a tool for improving future professional practice (this may include reflecting 'on' action or reflecting 'in' action).

- As a strategy for managing career development and promotion (this is considered in the final chapter of the book).

Identifying your preferred learning style

The work of Kolb (1984)

As Payne and Whittaker (2006) suggest, each of us is a unique individual and the way that we learn is therefore a matter of personal style, which may have been influenced by a whole range of factors, such as personal characteristics, life experience, upbringing and our peers. While it may therefore be true that no two people are exactly the same, many educators have attempted to categorise the main types of approach that an adult may use in order to learn. These are often referred to as learning styles. Here, we consider two theories that are among the most famous, and we start by returning to Kolb (1984). As discussed in Chapter 2, Kolb suggests that, unlike children, adults learn from experience and that this involves four stages. A reminder of what he refers to as the experiential learning cycle is provided here.

Learning starts with a *concrete experience* – in other words, an event that takes place. This is followed by *reflective observation,* a period during which we think over everything that happened during the event. The third stage is *abstract conceptualisation.* Put simply, this involves creating our own theory about the experience so that we may make sense of it. Finally, *active experimentation* involves testing the new theory in practice. However, Kolb (1984) goes on to suggest that although it is necessary to complete each element of the cycle in order to learn effectively, each learner has a natural preference for a particular part of the learning process and therefore places more emphasis upon it as their preferred learning style. Some learners therefore have what he refers to as an 'orientation'. In other words, some have a tendency towards learning through concrete experiences, some naturally prefer to learn through observing and reflecting, others have an orientation towards abstract conceptualisation or theorising, and some learn most easily through experimentation.

According to Kolb (1984), there are therefore four main learning styles that relate to a particular stage of the learning cycle. Each adult is more likely to approach their learning by using one of these stages more than the others.

The work of Honey and Mumford (1986)

Another very famous theory about adult learning styles is presented by Honey and Mumford (1986). Like Kolb, these theorists are frequently referred to in literature on education and learning, So you may have heard of them before, perhaps in other areas of your current educational programme such as 'study skills'. Honey and Mumford also use the four categories of learner identified according to Kolb's learning cycle but adapt the names of them so that they can be understood in a straightforward way. It is Honey and Mumford's learning styles that we consider in greater detail here.

Honey and Mumford suggest that some adults learn best by using the first part of the experiential learning cycle, the 'concrete experience' stage. These they refer to as *activist learners.* Some people have a tendency towards the second stage, 'reflective observation', and are therefore naturally *reflective learners.* Others favour stage three, which is 'abstract conceptualisation', and are what they refer to as *theorist learners.* Some people tend to learn best by using the last stage of the cycle, 'active experimentation', and they use the term *pragmatist learners* in order to describe them. The four learning styles and the stage of the learning cycle that they relate to are summarised in Table 6.1.

Table 6.1 Learning styles

Learning cycle stage	Learning style
Stage 1 Concrete experience	Activist
Stage 2 Reflective observation	Reflector
Stage 3 Abstract conceptualisation	Theorist
Stage 4 Active experimentation	Pragmatist

By considering each of these categories in turn, a description of each type of learner according to Honey and Mumford can be provided.

The activist

Activist learners can be thought of as the type of people who 'like to have a go' or have the attitude 'I'll try anything once' (Honey and Mumford, 1986, p5). They tend to enjoy new experiences and are therefore more concerned with trying out an activity rather than ensuring that it is fully completed. Activists are open-minded and enthusiastic about new situations but may become easily bored when required to put something into practice.

They enjoy excitement and may refer to themselves as 'sensation seekers'. Consider the example of learning how to ride a bicycle (although it may be assumed that this activity is often learned during childhood). The activist learner is likely to embrace the task and is happy to try, perhaps without considering the consequences of falling. They may, however, tire of practising and move on to the next activity.

The reflector

As identified in previous chapters, reflection usually involves thinking about situations that have taken place. Reflective learners are therefore usually regarded as thoughtful learners or 'thinkers'. Unlike activists, they tend to stand back from activities at first and consider the task from many angles. They usually prefer to understand the wider picture, including past experience and the present situation, before acting. They tend to be cautious by nature, and like to understand the meaning and implications of an activity before becoming involved. Often people who consider themselves to be very good listeners are reflective learners.

The theorist

The theorist is the type of learner who may often say 'Does it make sense?' (Honey and Mumford, 1986, p6). Theorist learners like to understand the principle of how something works rather than simply accepting that it does. They enjoy logic and like to work through an activity in a methodical way. They prefer certainty and feel uncomfortable with information that is subjective or 'vague'. You may recognise yourself as a theorist learner if you prefer to work to a clearly organised list. Individuals who have a background in science or mathematics often identify themselves as theorists.

The pragmatist

A pragmatist learner's main concern is 'Does it work?' Although they initially appear to be similar to activists, pragmatists are more concerned with 'getting the job done' than simply trying something out. They tend to take a practical, problem-solving approach to tasks and are sometimes intolerant of anything that may be regarded as 'waffle'. An expedition doctor may be considered as an example of a pragmatist. This is a medical expert who attends outdoor or even dangerous excursions. They may, for example, be able to treat someone with a broken limb using only the resources that are available at the time rather than the type of medical equipment usually found within a hospital setting.

PRACTICAL TASK

With a fellow student or friend, talk about the approach to a learning event that you are most likely to take. This could be a practical task such as learning to do something or perhaps your approach to learning when in a classroom environment. Describe the key characteristics of each learning style to the person and ask them what they have observed about the approach that they think describes you best. Then consider your own assessment of your preferred learning style. Do you feel that you are most like an activist, reflector, theorist or pragmatist?

A practical example: the flat-pack test

From the descriptions provided you may now have an idea of which learning style you are most suited to, and therefore how reflective you are currently as a learner. A further assessment may be made by considering how you might approach the task of putting together a piece of flat-pack furniture.

Imagine that you have returned home from a supermarket or furniture shop with a piece of furniture that needs to be built from a flat pack. The following represents the various approaches that may be taken when putting the item together according to the various learning styles.

- The activist learner may open the box with enthusiasm, excited by the challenge of constructing the object. He or she might 'dive in' without consulting the assembly instructions and only refer to them if unable to continue without them. There may, however, be a tendency to become frustrated and seek assistance with any problems that arise.

- The reflector may be more likely to think carefully about their approach to the task before starting. They may read the instructions and organise the pieces in the correct order. A cautious approach may be taken to ensuring that the object is correctly assembled, and this may take longer than the activist learner.

- The theorist learner might adopt a similar approach to the reflector; however, it is more likely that the process itself becomes more important than completing the task. He or she may make a detailed list of the actions to be taken and the correct sequence in which they should be completed. The theorist may enjoy discovering – or, indeed, feel that it is essential to understand – the logic of how the item is constructed before they can begin.

- The pragmatist might display less patience when completing the task. Their approach may be similar to the activist, however, as emphasis is placed upon completing the task and ensuring that it works. The instructions might be used; however, this may depend upon whether they are regarded as a practical necessity. Some educators jokingly suggest that the pragmatist may not undertake the task at all, but instead use an existing object as a substitute. As long as it 'gets the job done' it does not matter.

REFLECTIVE TASK

Consider the light-hearted example of learning how to construct a piece of furniture from a flat pack and the approaches that may be taken. Consider your own approach. If you have not attempted this in the past, think about how you might attempt it. Which learning style do you feel best describes you?

*You may also wish to complete the learning styles questionnaire provided by Honey and Mumford (1986) in order to explore your learning style in greater detail. Information relating to this is available at the Peter Honey website at **www.peterhoney.com**. There may, however, be a charge for accessing the questionnaire via the website. A paper version may be obtained from* The Manual of Learning Styles *(Honey and Mumford, 1986).*

REFLECTIVE TASK *continued*

This may be available from the library at your learning environment, and the reference for this is listed at the end of the chapter.

It is worth noting that the approach taken when undertaking this task may in itself provide a further example of the learning style that you have a tendency towards. Consider the actions that you took. Which learning style are they most associated with?

The all-round learner

As indicated above, the main aim of this chapter is to provide a range of techniques designed to assist you in taking a reflective approach to your learning, not only during your current studies but as a 'future way of life'. By doing this it is possible to become the type of lifelong learner discussed in previous chapters. Some strategies for assisting you in strengthening your reflective learning style are therefore provided in the second part of this chapter. Before doing so, however, it is useful to briefly consider the advantages of strengthening each of the other learning styles.

Honey and Mumford (1986) suggest that the ideal learner not only understands their preferred learning style but also is able to develop each of the other three in order to become an all-round learner. It is possible to think of this as having a 'bag of tricks' from which the best learning approach can be chosen depending upon the circumstances. We list here some of the specific situations in which an activist, theorist or pragmatist approach may be appropriate.

Using the correct learning style

The activist approach
This approach to learning is useful in situations that require immediate action. In the classroom, for example, activist learners are often more outspoken than theorist learners because they are happy to try out ideas, even if they are unsuccessful. They may be less self-conscious about contributing an opinion and learn by experimenting when engaging in conversations.

This learning approach may also be useful on some occasions during your future policing career. An emergency situation may require you to act immediately, perhaps if someone's life is threatened. Hesitation may be inappropriate or even dangerous.

Improving your activist style
- Consider adopting a new hobby. Doing this may assist you in trying new activities and adapting to unfamiliar situations.

- Where appropriate, try initiating conversations more often. This may be with someone you have not spoken to before, or it could involve offering your opinion in the learning environment. This may help you to become more spontaneous as a learner.

The theorist approach

For some situations, immediate action may be less desirable. The theorist style is useful when approaching a task that requires careful analysis or thought. An example of this may be when preparing an academic argument for a particular assignment. The ability to use analysis in order to critically evaluate a theory may be useful here.

During your future policing career, there may also be occasions that require thorough and thoughtful planning – an undercover policing operation, for example. In this type of situation it is immediate action that would be dangerous.

Improving your theorist style

- When reading textbooks, practise asking yourself critical questions about the material. You may even wish to write these down. Think about what a theory may mean and if there are any alternative ways that it can be understood.

- Consider taking a very organised approach to your daily activities or studies. Perhaps you might start to make detailed lists of tasks that need to be undertaken and in what order.

The pragmatist approach

Pragmatist learners are generally regarded as effective 'finishers'. This style of learning approach is therefore helpful for ensuring that tasks are completed. This may be useful for ensuring that assessment deadlines are met, for example.

Alternatively, the ability to be pragmatic – in other words, 'practical' – will have obvious advantages for you during your policing career. In a similar way to the example of the expedition doctor discussed earlier, there may be situations that require you to act with very few resources available to you. An example of this may be a traffic accident at which you are the first person on the scene. It could be necessary to assist a casualty in the street before medical assistance arrives.

Improving your pragmatist style

- Practise setting clear deadlines for activities that you intend to complete. You may wish to combine this with the theorist task of list making. By doing this it is possible to decide what tasks need to be undertaken and the deadline for completion.

- Engage in a practical task. Again, you may wish to combine this with the activist task of undertaking a hobby. It may be possible to choose an activity that involves learning how to make something, such as woodwork classes or card making.

PRACTICAL TASK

For each of the learning styles – activist, theorist, pragmatist – write down a recent learning event in which the learning might have been the most appropriate. The events may relate to your current studies or an experience in your personal life in which you learned something new. Then make some notes in relation to the following questions.

PRACTICAL TASK *continued*

1 Which of these situations was most successful for me?

2 Which was the least successful?

3 Which learning styles would I like to develop and improve?

Finally, compile a list of activities that might help you to strengthen these styles. The key thing is to ensure that these are achievable and realistic.

Reflective learning: strategies for strengthening your reflective learning style

We now return to the idea that reflection is a state of mind (Bolton, 2010). There will undoubtedly be occasions when the ability to adopt an activist, theorist or pragmatist learning style may be useful. The main purpose of this book, however, is to consider the use of reflection as a lifelong skill that can assist your learning both currently and during your future career, so here we consider a range of strategies to assist you in strengthening this ability. You may have already identified a tendency towards reflective learning and therefore wish only to further develop this. For some learners, however, reflective thinking may feel less natural, and they will therefore require a greater amount of practice. As discussed earlier, it is possible to think of this as a form of mind training similar to any other form of exercise. We start by considering the advantages of planning your reflective time.

Creating reflective time

In Chapter 4 we briefly considered the importance of creating time to be reflective. Many of us have very busy lives with all sorts of commitments and responsibilities. Even professionals who are required to engage in reflective practice, such as nurses, sometimes suggest that they only find the opportunity to reflect when driving home from work or when relaxing in the bath. If possible, however, it is helpful to take an organised approach to reflective practice by allocating dedicated time. This will inevitably depend upon personal circumstance and may involve a short period of daily reflection, or perhaps a longer session once or even twice per week. If you are able, it is important to ensure that this is a period of quiet time with as few distractions as possible. By doing this it may be possible to capture some of the thoughts and reflections that you have as you go about your daily life. It may also be useful to write down some of your reflections rather than merely thinking about them, so we now consider the value of reflective writing.

Consider the time that you have available to you for reflecting. If it is helpful, you may wish to compile a weekly timetable of the activities that require completion. You may have already been invited to create a study timetable during your current learning. Make a plan that provides an outline of the following.

1 How often will I allow time to reflect?

2 How long will I reflect for during each session?

3 Where will I reflect?

4 Are there any particular arrangements that I could make in order to allow time for my reflections?

Reflective writing

Jasper (2003) provides the following definition: 'Reflective writing involves engaging in and completing the reflective cycle using written processes to help you learn' (p143). She further suggests that this is a particularly useful activity because it requires reflection to be undertaken in a conscious and deliberate way. Moon (2004) makes the point that writing takes place at a slower pace than thinking. It therefore provides extra time to work through ideas and arrive at successful conclusions. Reflective writing also produces a record of learning and development that can be referred back to. According to Bolton (2010), there are many forms of reflective writing, including note taking and learning journals. Perhaps one of the most common is reflective diaries.

Reflective diaries

At some point during your life you may have chosen to keep a personal diary as a hobby. Diaries are often regarded as a therapeutic means of expressing thoughts and feelings and making a permanent record of your memories. In a very similar way it is possible to complete a learning diary. Here Borton's (1970) reflective model (or indeed any of the other models that have been considered) may be used as a guide to your reflective writing in exactly the same way as the type of reflective thinking described in earlier chapters. You may consider writing either a paragraph, or listing some points in note form for each element of the reflective model. This type of exercise has several specific advantages identified by Moon (2004).

- Reflective writing using the models that you have been introduced to can be regarded as 'works in progress'. In other words, it is possible to revisit particular reflections on several occasions, building upon them, changing your opinion, and arriving at new conclusions about how to respond in future situations.

- As suggested earlier, a diary provides a permanent record of your learning journey. This may be simply for your own reference, or it can be used to provide evidence of your development and progress to an employer in the future. In the modern world, employers are becoming increasingly interested in staff who can demonstrate that they are lifelong learners (we consider this in more detail in the next chapter).

- Learning diaries provide a private opportunity to express the types of personal feelings and emotions that you may not wish to discuss with others. When using Borton's model, therefore, the 'So what?' element may be used to write down how a situation made you feel. This way the reflective process can be used in a therapeutic way which may be very helpful during periods of stress or uncertainty.

A final benefit of maintaining a reflective diary is the opportunity to create an action plan. Having completed the last part of Borton's reflective model – 'Now what?' – you may have identified the type of actions that could assist you in dealing with future situations more effectively. This may be a general decision such as 'I will be more assertive in future' or 'I would like to appear more confident in a similar situation'. Alternatively, you may have considered a detailed or specific set of measures that you would like to take. Written reflection provides an opportunity to produce an action plan so that you can implement these actions in a systematic way. You may consider including the following.

- What would I like to do?

- How will I approach this?

- In what order will I complete this?

- What is my personal deadline for completion?

PRACTICAL TASK

Make yourself a reflective diary or journal from a notebook. You may be able to purchase one cheaply, or use a spare pad of paper that you already possess. During the time that you allocated in the last practical task, write down your reflections. You may use Borton's model as a guide (or one of the other models, such as Driscoll (2000) or Gibbs (1998), considered in Chapter 4).

Concept mapping

Another tool that may assist you with reflection is concept mapping. Reflective models are a very useful guide when breaking down the process of reflection into simple parts. Some situations, however, may be more straightforward than others to reflect upon. On some occasions you may have a very clear understanding of everything that took place and the actions that may be taken during similar events in the future. Others may be far more complicated, or your recollection of them may be unclear. Thompson and Thompson (2008) suggest that a concept map is a visual tool that helps not only to break down large complex ideas but also to recognise the connections between them. This is because people do not usually think in a linear way – in other words, in a straight line that moves from 'A' to 'B'. Rather, there is a tendency to jump backwards and forwards from one idea to another. A map more accurately shows how separate ideas may be 'dotted about' but have particular links between them, rather like a map in which towns are connected together by roads.

When reflecting upon a complicated situation, it may therefore be helpful to begin by drawing a concept map in order to organise muddled thoughts into a clear and logical order. This can assist you in deciding upon the most important issues for each stage of the reflective cycle (What? So what? Now what?). An example of how you might complete a concept map using Borton's reflective model is provided.

Drawing a concept map

Start with a blank piece of paper that is laid out in the 'landscape' position (with the longest side at the top). You may wish to use a page from your reflective diary for this. Write a title in the centre of the paper that refers to the situation you wish to reflect upon and draw a circle around it. Here, we consider the example of giving evidence in court.

Draw three lines that branch out from the circle and label them 'What?', 'So what?' and 'Now what?', as shown in the next diagram.

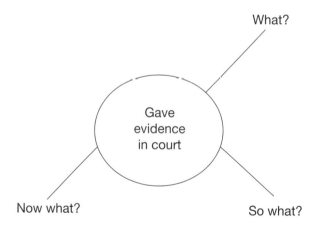

At the end of the 'What?' branch, draw smaller lines and label them with the most important things about the event. You might consider the following.

- What happened?

- What went well?

- What did I not do so well?

Again, a diagram is provided.

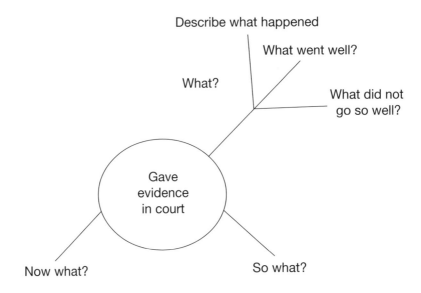

Repeat the process for the 'So what?' branch, this time recording your impressions of what the event meant, what the implications were and perhaps how it made you feel. You may wish to include things such as the following.

- So what is my assessment?

- So what was the result?

- How well do I think I represented myself, personally and as a professional?

Finally, against the 'Now what?' branch consider any actions that you could take in a similar situation. For each line you may wish to sub divide further still in order to include more detail against each item. There may, for example, be an action point that has two parts to it. This may involve things such as the following.

- The things that you would repeat.

- The things that you would do differently.

- The actions that you may need to take in order to assist you in acting differently. This may, for example, involve taking advice from a more experienced colleague.

An example of a completed concept map is provided.

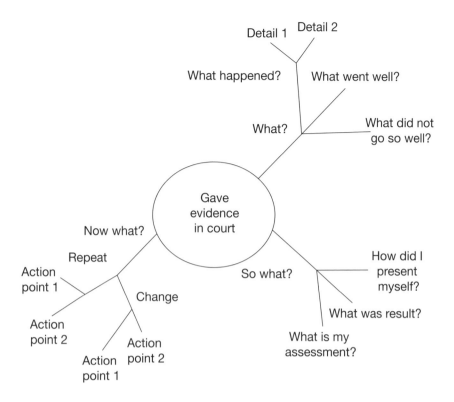

PRACTICAL TASK

Using the description above, reflect upon a recent situation using a concept map.

Emotional intelligence

It is useful to briefly consider the importance of emotion when developing reflective skills. Chapter 3 considered the role of values and beliefs in reflective learning. Very closely related to this is the idea of emotional intelligence. So far, a practical approach has been taken to developing your reflective ability. While there is no doubt that a practical, problem-solving approach is helpful, it should also be acknowledged that our behaviour, the actions of others and, indeed, the reflections that we have upon various situations are often motivated by our feelings. (These may, in turn, be influenced by the types of values and beliefs that were identified in Chapter 3.) Here, we consider the merits of understanding what emotional intelligence is, and how it may strengthen your ability to reflect in an effective way.

Thompson and Thompson (2008, p41) provide a very simple definition: 'Being tuned in to other people's feelings as well as our own is precisely what emotional intelligence is all about.' This refers to the ability to interpret subtle messages about the emotional state of another individual that may be contained within their tone of voice, their choice of words or their actions. It is possible to think of these as a series of 'clues' that indicate not only how the person feels but also how these feelings may motivate them to behave in a particular way. Whether it is during your current studies or as a future police officer, there will be very few situations that do not involve at least some form of human interaction (even writing an essay is likely to involve a discussion with a tutor or a fellow student at some point). Unlike machines, people do not usually perform in a logical and straight-forward way. Rather, behaviour is often unpredictable and complex, and may be influenced by all sorts of factors that are not immediately obvious, such as insecurity, fear or perhaps even over-confidence. The ability to understand emotion is therefore very useful when reflecting upon situations, particularly those that are complicated. It allows for a much broader understanding of not only what happened but also *why* it happened. Understanding these types of complexities may allow for a much richer type of reflection. It also provides an opportunity to consider the implications of any future actions upon the emotional well-being of others. This may be true when considering your own emotions, too, and how they influenced your behaviour in a particular situation.

Unlike some tools, Borton's reflective model does not specifically prompt the reflector to consider feelings and emotions; however, it can easily be incorporated into the 'What?' or 'So what?' elements of the model. It is helpful, therefore, when reflecting, to routinely consider the role that your own emotions or the feelings of others may have played in a particular situation, by using either a diary or a concept map. It should be emphasised that being emotionally intelligent, rather like reflection itself, is a skill that develops over a long period of time through practice and experience. It therefore cannot be learned instantly but may improve slowly by incorporating it into your reflective activities.

PRACTICAL TASK

Think about a recent situation that you would like to reflect upon and decide whether you wish to think about it, write it down or produce a concept map. Using Borton's model, include the following.

- *What?*
  - *What were your own feelings?*
  - *What 'clues' did you notice about the feelings of others?*
  - *What was their influence upon the behaviour of others?*
- *So what?*
  - *So what influence may these have had upon the situation?*
  - *So what were the implications of them for the outcome of the situation?*
- *Now what?*
  - *Now what actions could I take as a result of understanding these emotions?*
  - *Now what might the effects of these actions be upon the emotional well-being of others (if any).*

Adopting an enquiring attitude

As an adult you will undoubtedly have a certain amount of knowledge learned from experience. It is possible, however, to think of oneself as 'work in progress' rather than the finished article. By adopting an open-minded, enquiring approach to learning, most situations can become an opportunity to make new discoveries. This may be thought of as rather like a small infant who constantly asks 'Why?' Bolton (2010) suggests that becoming reflective as a learner involves adapting our general attitude so that we accept the following three principles.

- *Certain uncertainty* She suggests that the only thing about which we can be certain is that the world is full of uncertainties rather than definite answers. Learning can therefore be a creative process in which we accept that many things are unknown but are waiting to be discovered.

- *Serious playfulness* This suggests that learning may be regarded as an adventure in which we experiment with ideas. It is important to stress, however, that your current learning and, in particular, your future career as a police officer carries with it a large amount of responsibility and should therefore be taken seriously. The serious element, therefore, according to Bolton, involves adopting a playful approach in a responsible way, and within a safe learning environment rather than in a professional practice situation.

- *Unquestioning questioning* It is suggested that the adult learner adopts a non-judgemental and questioning approach to the world rather than simply accepting taking ideas for granted.

Reflecting in pairs

Peer reflection

So far we have considered the types of activities that may help you improve your reflective learning style. These, however, have centred upon reflection as an individual activity. It is also useful to consider how working with others can assist you in becoming more reflective. In Chapter 2 we considered a professional activity referred to as 'clinical supervision'. This is usually a formal relationship in which a supervisor regularly assists a member of staff in reflecting upon their practice (Jasper, 2003). While this has been a compulsory requirement for healthcare professionals for many years, it does not currently apply to policing staff (or, indeed, students). It may be useful to be aware of this, however, not only because of future changes that may take place within policing but also because of the benefits of creating your own informal version. It is possible to think of this as a 'buddy' system (Thompson and Thompson, 2008).

Reflecting with a fellow student or, in the future, a professional colleague may have the following advantages.

- It can be used as a therapeutic way of talking about complicated or even traumatic events.

- It supports the saying 'two heads are better than one' and can therefore be used as a way of exploring solutions to problems with someone who has a different perspective.

- Your reflection 'buddy' may prompt you with each stage of a reflective cycle, particularly when you are learning reflection as a new skill.

- It is sometimes easier to clarify thoughts by speaking them out loud.

Consider approaching a friend or another student in your learning group and asking them if they would like to become your reflection buddy. They may have some prior knowledge of reflective practice. If not, it may be an opportunity to explain the benefits of reflection to them. Arrange a regular time and place for your reflective sessions. During these sessions, work through a reflective model together, perhaps Borton (1970). Your buddy may read out each stage of the model and prompt you with your answers in order to clarify meaning. It is helpful to be aware that these types of reflective sessions often become an opportunity to offload feelings and vent frustrations. While this can be helpful, it is important to ensure that each stage of the model is completed, particularly the final element. This is to ensure that you reach a conclusion that assists your development, rather than that you simply engage in an informal conversation. You may wish to record your reflections in your diary after the session so that you have a permanent record of them.

Personal tutorials

Other opportunities for reflecting in pairs are your 'one-to-one' tutorials with your personal tutor. It is likely that you already undertake regular tutorials as part of your current learning programme. If you wish, you may talk to your tutor about reflective practice and request that some of your tutorial time is used to work through areas of your development using a reflective model.

PRACTICAL TASK

Complete one of the following activities.

- *Identify a student in your learning group that you have a good relationship with. Ask them if they would like to become your reflection buddy. Arrange a time and a place for your first meeting.*

- *Talk to your personal tutor about reflective practice. Ask if a reflective approach could be taken to your personal tutorial so that areas for personal development may be identified.*

PRACTICAL TASK

Knowledge check review

Revisit the questions listed here. Then compare them with your answers at the beginning of the chapter in order to assess your learning.

- *What are the uses of reflection within adult learning?*

PRACTICAL TASK *continued*

- *To what extent do I consciously use reflective practice in order to enhance my learning?*
- *What strategies could I consider for strengthening my ability to reflect?*

C H A P T E R   S U M M A R Y

This chapter has considered the many uses of reflective practice and the benefits of improving your reflective abilities. It has introduced the range of learning styles according to Kolb (1984) and Honey and Mumford (1986). An opportunity to identify your own learning preference was provided. The chapter then introduced a series of strategies that may be used in order to assist you in becoming more reflective as a learner. You should now have a better understanding of how to strengthen your reflective learning style.

FURTHER READING

The manual of learning styles (Honey and Mumford, 1986) provides a detailed description of the four learning styles considered within the chapter. A learning style questionnaire is provided in order to enable students to diagnose their learning style.

REFERENCES

Bolton, G (2010) *Reflective practice, writing and professional development*, 3rd edition. London: Sage.

Borton, T (1970) *Reach, teach and touch*. London: McGraw Hill.

Honey, P and Mumford, A (1986) *The manual of learning styles*, 2nd edition. Maidenhead: Peter Honey.

Jasper, M (2003) *Beginning reflective practice*. Cheltenham: Nelson Thornes.

Kolb, D (1984) *Experiential learning: experience as a source of learning and development*. Saddle River NJ: Prentice Hall.

Moon, J (2004) *Reflection in learning and professional development*. Oxford: Routledge Falmer.

Payne, E and Whittaker, L (2006) *Developing essential study skills*, 2nd edition. London: Prentice Hall.

Thompson, S and Thompson, N (2008) *The critically reflective practitioner*. Basingstoke: Palgrave Macmillan.

USEFUL WEBSITES

www.peterhoney.com/(Honey and Mumford's learning style questionnaire)

7 Reflecting for life: planning a successful career

Introduction

This chapter considers the potential uses of reflection during the various stages of your future career development. Four broad areas are considered.

- The adult lifelong learner.

- Starting your career.

- Developing your professional practice as a police officer.

- Future promotion.

It starts by revisiting the idea of lifelong learning in the modern world of employment. The term 'employability' is introduced and you are invited to assess your skills and qualities for future employment. The chapter then outlines a range of strategies for developing and enhancing your professional practice as a police officer by reflecting 'on' action and reflecting 'in' action. The use of the Performance and Development Review (PDR) process for career development is then considered. Finally, the chapter examines the use of reflection for planning future promotion. We start with a knowledge check, a series of questions designed to assess your current understanding of how reflection may be used in order to maximise your future success. You are invited to revisit these at the end of the chapter in order to measure your learning.

PRACTICAL TASK

Knowledge check

On a piece of paper or perhaps in your reflective diary, jot down your answers to the following questions.

- *What do I know about the importance of lifelong learning for my future career?*
- *What do I think the term 'employability' means?*
- *What type of skills am I developing for future employability?*
- *What can I remember about reflecting 'on' and reflecting 'in' action?*
- *How might they help me improve my practice as a future police officer?*
- *What do I think a Performance and Development Review might be?*
- *How might reflection help me to plan and achieve promotion in the future?*

The adult 'lifelong learner'

Chapter 1 explored some of the most significant developments within adult education since the election of the Labour government in 1997. These related not only to educational policy in general but also to the specific changes to police training and education considered within the documents *Managing learning* (O'Dowd, 1999) and *Training matters* (Home Office, 2002). A key theme that reappeared throughout many of these documents was a commitment to the term 'lifelong learning'. We consider this in greater detail here. By doing this you may gain a better understanding of what may be expected of you in the future as an employee.

According to Morgan-Kleine and Osborne (2007), the current emphasis upon lifelong learning is far from new; in fact, it developed during the 1980s and 1990s as a response to globalism. The term 'globalism' refers to the manner in which countries have become increasingly interconnected by technology, transport and improved methods of communication, and how this has resulted in much higher levels of international competition. As considered in Chapter 1, many of the developments brought about by the Labour government in the late 1990s aimed to ensure that Britain could compete, particularly with very powerful countries within the international labour market. A key element of this was the development of a highly skilled workforce.

The modern workplace therefore demands employees who have increased levels of train-ing and education in order to perform their role. This is one of the main reasons that higher educational programmes are now encouraged for many occupations, including policing. There is also, however, an emphasis placed upon what is referred to as lifelong learning – in other words, learning that continues throughout the course of an individual's life (Spurling, 1995). This, as Morgan-Kleine and Osborne (2007) suggest, is due to a world of rapid technological change and a labour market in which 'lifetime employment in one career or job is no longer the norm' (p84). A particular set of skills is not sufficient for the whole of an individual's career; a flexible approach to learning, development and acquir-ing new skills, sometimes referred to as 'up skilling', is required instead .

Here, we place this in the context of your future policing career as an example. At some point in the future, having graduated from your current learning programme, you may be successfully recruited as a police officer. You will therefore not only have a high standard of academic knowledge and ability but also be provided with the practical skills required to perform in your role effectively. It is unlikely, however, that these skills could simply be repeated for the whole of your career. Technology, such as the equipment or computer systems that you use, will change, as will local and national policies, laws and social attitudes. You may also wish to work towards promotion, or a particular policing spe-ciality, such as the Underwater Search Team or the Firearms and Explosives Unit. Any of these changes may require you to think differently or undertake further training so that your knowledge and skills remain up to date.

Equally, your abilities when performing particular tasks will gradually improve over a period of time. The manner in which you attend to a distressed member of the public with a mental illness, for example, may be very different at the start of your career from the approach taken after 20 years of policing experience. In many respects, learning will therefore be a continuous or lifelong process.

There are two things that are implied within the above examples. First, specific training and educational programmes should be provided for employees so that their skills can continue to develop throughout their employment. This type of formal learning input is the responsibility of the employer. Second, however, the staff member is required to take a developmental approach to their own career. This involves actively participating in learning opportunities, applying new knowledge to practical situations, and improving personal performance using reflection. Lifelong learning is therefore a shared responsibility between the work establishment and the employee (Fullick, 2004).

Lifelong learning and reflection

Previous chapters have considered the importance of reflection for adult learning. Because learning is an ongoing process, reflection will continue to play a vital role within your career and, indeed, personal development. Chapter 6 considered a range of methods designed to assist you in developing a reflective approach to learning as a 'state of mind'. This chapter considers strategies that may help you consciously plan and take respon-sibility for your future career development using your new reflective abilities.

Starting your career

Employability

Very closely related to the idea of lifelong learning is what is often referred to as 'employability'. Dacre Pool and Sewell (2007) suggest that for many the term is often misunderstood and assumed to refer simply to securing employment or 'getting a job' (p277). A more accurate description of employability, however, is the development of the correct skills for long-term employment. Payne and Whittaker (2006) suggest that employers increasingly aim to recruit staff that possess a variety of skills that include the ability to adapt and learn. Some of these skills are listed here.

- Personal motivation.

- Willingness to develop and learn.

- The ability to be critical and reflective.

- Reliability.

- Effective time management.

- Flexibility.

Consider your current learning. It is likely that you have been introduced to many theories that may assist you within your future policing role. Some of these, such as diversity issues, were considered in Chapter 5 when exploring the role of reflection for relating theory to practice. The act of studying in itself, however, also provides a range of skills that are desirable to future employers, including the police service. We consider some of these here.

Writing skills
There may be occasions when essay writing feels like a difficult art to learn. Some students find this frustrating at times, especially if their aim is to undertake a practical role such as policing. However, the advantage – for you and your future employer – is that you may have improved your ability to communicate effectively in writing. Chapter 1 considered the Skills for Life strategy (2001), in which the need to improve standards of English and maths among British adults was identified. Graduate employees benefit from having the ability to present professionally written documentation in a variety of situations – report writing, for example.

Verbal communication
Equally, during your current studies it is likely that you have been required to deliver individual or group presentations as a form of assessment. You may also have become increasingly confident when expressing your point of view or defending an argument in group discussions. Although these types of situation may feel uncomfortable or perhaps even stressful, they will undoubtedly assist you in developing your verbal communication skills. The value of this for future employment is the ability to present yourself confidently to a variety of different audiences. Your future work may involve liaising very closely with a wide range of people – managers, colleagues and various members of the public, for

example. The ability to communicate with others in an effective manner is a transferable skill that can increase your desirability as an employee generally, and assist your performance in a variety of situations as a police officer, such as giving evidence in court or liaising with the general public.

Autonomy

This term refers to the ability to make personal decisions and act independently. Earlier chapters identified some of the differences between childhood and adult learning. Children usually require structured settings in which the teacher assumes responsibility for the pupil's education. During your current studies your learning is more likely to be self-directed and involve a lesser degree of supervision. For example, there is much greater emphasis placed upon learning independently, effective time management in order to observe set deadlines, and personal motivation and self-discipline. All of these qualities strengthen the ability to take responsibility for your personal actions in the future. If we consider this in the context of policing practice, there will be situations in which there are strict procedural guidelines to follow. On many occasions, however, the manner in which you manage your own practice will be a matter of personal discretion, such as how you organise your time and workload. Many of the skills acquired during your current learning programme may therefore contribute to the ability to take responsibility for work practices and, indeed, your own career development in the future.

Problem solving

In a similar way, your studies can provide an opportunity to strengthen your problem-solving skills. This may relate to the ability to analyse theoretical material in a critical way. Often, however, adult educational programmes require the student to find solutions to problems that relate to the process of studying itself. This may include things such as deciding upon priorities for studying, balancing your studies with other areas of your life, or simply managing unexpected personal problems that might affect your learning. Developing an ability to cope with these challenges may help you to think creatively, be flexible and use your own initiative. These types of skills will no doubt be of use to you during your future employment, particularly in a role such as policing, which often requires the ability to find solutions to complicated situations.

Reflecting upon employability – identifying your transferable skills

Previous chapters have discussed the many benefits of reflection for personal and professional development. The next section considers the ways that it may be used in order to enhance and improve your professional performance throughout your future career as a police officer and lifelong learner. Here, we pause briefly in order to explore the use of reflection for identifying the range of skills that you already possess or are developing during your studies, some of which you may not be consciously aware of. These are often referred to as transferable skills because they are the kinds of qualities that can be used or recycled in a variety of different situations. This is a very useful exercise because it may enable you to be confident about the skills that you bring to the police service as you embark upon your career journey and about the many things that make you employable as a police officer.

Valuing yourself

The process of reflection, particularly reflecting on action, often requires you to think critically about your own performance. Chapter 2 considered the potential for this type of self-analysis to be misinterpreted as a negative process of self-criticism. Instead, it should be thought of as a means of considering solutions to situations or problems in a balanced way. This may therefore sometimes involve acknowledging your strengths as well as your weaknesses. One very positive use of reflection in relation to employability is the opportunity to recognise and take pride in the many skills that you have developed. Although there may be a significant period of time before you complete your current learning programme, you may wish to regularly reflect upon your progress, perhaps using your reflective diary. At the end of your studies this may assist you in presenting yourself to a future employer or applying to the police service with confidence in your value as a future employee. The advantages of this approach are listed below.

- An awareness of your skills for employment.

- An understanding of your weaknesses and an opportunity to improve upon them as early as possible.

- An opportunity to recognise the particular skills required for a policing career and build upon them.

- The ability to promote your skills when writing a curriculum vitae (CV).

- A similar ability to identify and demonstrate your competencies during the police application process.

This may help you not only to develop confidence and self-esteem but also to adopt a strategic approach to developing your skills. You may think of this as gathering your own tools for future employability.

PRACTICAL TASK

Complete the following exercise. Either make a list, or create a concept map of the types of activities that police officers may undertake. You may have explored some of these during your current learning. Alternatively, it may be helpful to visit the police recruitment website www.policecouldyou.co.uk/ and explore the sections relating to 'Police officers'.

Now reflect upon the transferable skills that you are developing or already possess. Consider each of the following.

- *What skills might be important as a police officer?*

- *Which of these do you already possess?*

- *Why might these skills be important?*

- *Are there any skills that you are lacking?*

- *How might you develop these skills?*

Finally, write a list of the transferable skills that you have for employment and an action plan for the skills that you would like to improve upon.

Developing your professional practice as a police officer

Reflecting on action

Here, we consider the use of reflection for improving your professional practice during your future policing career. This may feel strange because you are being invited to think into the future. Professional reflection, however, will involve very similar thinking skills to those that you have developed and started to use during your learning. The advantage of a reflective approach to your practice is that you can take responsibility for continually learning and improving as you progress throughout your career, rather than simply repeating your training several times. This way, you become your own independent theorist because, as discussed in Chapter 2, you have learned how to learn. This is one of the crucial aspects of lifelong learning considered earlier. Here, some examples of future policing situations are provided for you to practise reflecting. These have been designed to fit with some of the priorities for modern policing identified in Chapter 5 – they relate to community policing, equality and diversity issues and the needs of victims.

REFLECTIVE TASK

Scenario 1

Consider the following situation. As a newly qualified police officer you are called to a disagreement outside a house between two neighbours. One is accusing the other of playing loud music late in the evening. You talk calmly to both individuals; however, one becomes agitated and threatens the other. You therefore call for assistance and make an arrest for threatening behaviour.

Reflect upon the above situation using Borton's (1970) reflective model. By now you may feel confident enough to attempt this independently; alternatively, you may wish to use the following types of question as a prompt.

- *What happened in this situation?*

- *What did I do?*

- *What did others do?*

- *What was the outcome?*

- *So what did this mean?*

- *What is my interpretation of the situation?*

- *Now what action might I take in the future?*

- *Now what might I repeat in a future situation?*

- *Now what could I do differently?*

REFLECTIVE TASK continued

As part of your reflections you may consider some additional factors. For example, might your knowledge of social and criminological theory have helped you understand this situation? This was referred to in Chapter 5 as relating theory to practice. Is there anything else that you could plan to do in order to successfully manage a similar situation? You might consider obtaining advice from a more senior colleague or asking for a particular type of training, for example.

REFLECTIVE TASK

Scenario 2

You are discussing a particular incident with a colleague in the staff room. They make a comment about a member of the public that you do not agree with. This may relate to the age or gender of the person, for example. You decide to challenge this; however, your colleague becomes annoyed and leaves the room.

Consider the above example. You may wish to reflect upon it using Borton's (1970) model. The same types of question suggested for Scenario 1 may be useful. Borton's model has been referred to in previous chapters because it is a relatively simple way of getting started with reflection. If you wish, however, you may experiment with a more detailed model such as Gibbs (1988). A description of this was also provided in Chapter 4. One advantage of this model is that it specifically prompts the reflector to consider their thoughts and feelings during the event (although it is still possible to do this using the 'What?' stage of Borton's model). As discussed in Chapter 3, our feelings often influence our actions and this may involve the values and beliefs that we bring to a situation. Gibbs's model offers a useful opportunity to remember to consider these. The types of question that you may ask are listed here.

- *What took place?*

- *What were your thoughts and feelings?*

- *What worked well or not so well?*

- *What is your analysis? Or, in other words, what is your interpretation here?*

- *What else might have been done?*

- *What action could be taken if a similar situation arose?*

REFLECTIVE TASK

Scenario 3

You attend to a reported crime against an elderly member of the community. They tell you that they have been the victim of a burglary; however, their description of events appears to be somewhat confused. The house was apparently empty at the time of the incident and you are unable to find any evidence that a burglary has taken place.

For this scenario, choose the model that you prefer in order to assist you in reflecting upon it. Also consider some of the measures that you might take in the future in order to manage your reflections in a structured way. You might consider some of the following.

- *When will I reflect following a particular event?*

Would it be best to reflect immediately afterwards, for example? Alternatively, would you prefer to dedicate regular time for reflection? If so, depending upon your circumstances, how often would be best, ideally?

- *How will I reflect?*

Do you think it would suit you best simply to think about your reflections or would you prefer to record them? If so, could you plan to keep a reflective diary?

- *Do I reflect best on my own?*

You may consider whether you would prefer to reflect privately or with others. As a future police officer, you may decide, for example, to find a colleague who can become your reflection buddy so that you can assist each other's development.

Reflecting in action

Of the various uses for reflection, perhaps the one that has been considered least is reflecting 'in' action. While it is true that most situations can be analysed afterwards, there may be occasions when important yet rapid decisions or assessments need to take place during the event – reflection on action may simply be too late. Reflecting in action may therefore assist you in the future when thinking through important decisions quickly. Although many commentators suggest ways in which this may be undertaken, you can use Borton's model again here. As considered in Chapter 4, due to its simplicity this model can be carried around in your head and remembered very easily, even when under a certain amount of pressure.

REFLECTIVE TASK

Think of a policing situation in which you may need to make a decision quickly and write down a description of it. Some ideas are provided in order to help you.

- *A public meeting with a community group in which some of the members become angry.*

- *An emergency situation.*

- *Dealing with a victim of a crime who is very tearful and distressed.*

Think about the things that you might consider while the situation is taking place.

- *What is happening here?*

- *So what does it mean?*

- *What might happen?*

- *What are the dangers?*

- *What are my options?*

- *Now what could I do?*

- *Now what will I do?*

Looking after yourself

There is no doubt that your future role will be both rewarding and demanding. Here, we briefly consider some tips for taking a reflective approach to various aspects of your working life in order to maintain your own well-being as well as making the most of your career.

Recognising pressure and stress

Bingham and Drew (1999) suggest that pressure can build up without an individual being fully aware of it. This may be especially true for roles that are often very stressful, such as policing. It is important, therefore, to recognise the signs of pressure and stress so that they can be managed early. However, these signs, as well as the causes, will vary according to the person. Some people thrive on exciting situations, for example; as discussed in Chapter 6, people who consider themselves to be 'activist' in their approach to learning may be included here. Others, however, find these types of situation much more stressful. It is helpful, therefore, to identify the signs that you are under large amounts of pressure by reflecting upon past experiences. By doing this you may develop a sense of not only what the warning signs may be for you but also which types of situation tend to lead to them.

Think back to a time in your life when you considered yourself to have been under pressure. Reflect upon this by considering the following.

- *What was the situation or series of events?*

- *What was the cause of this pressure for you?*

- *What did this mean for you?*
- *What did it feel like?*
- *What did you do in order to relieve this?*
- *What could you do in future situations in order to reduce the pressure upon you?*

Managing stress

There are many strategies that may assist you in managing stress during your future career; some of them will develop with experience, and may depend upon your personal preferences. It is likely, however, that engagement in regular reflection will be helpful. You may therefore wish to develop the habit of regularly assessing your stress levels when you reflect, perhaps when considering how situations made you feel. Sometimes simply working out a solution to a problem helps to reduce feelings of stress or potential anxiety.

There may, however, be other practical measures that you can take. In the next section we consider effective time management and work–life balance. You may also consider ensuring that you find time outside work to take part in the things that you enjoy, such as a hobby or spending time with family. Bingham and Drew (1999) also suggest that regular participation in a sport helps to break down the build-up of hormones associated with stress – as well as being a pleasurable activity. A healthy diet and adequate sleep are useful for maintaining a healthy immune system and reducing the likelihood of stress-related illness.

PRACTICAL TASK

On a piece of paper or perhaps in your reflective diary, make an action plan of at least two things that you may do, either as a student or in the future as a police officer, in order to manage your stress levels. Consider what you may do, why you think it may be helpful and any specific arrangements that you may need to make.

Managing your time

As a student, you may be consciously aware that you have a limited amount of disposable income; you may plan your finances carefully and perhaps be cautious about your spending. Often, however, individuals do not apply the same discipline when organising their time. It is possible to think of your time as a limited resource that requires you to budget the amount that you spend. By doing so, you may be able to maintain a work–life balance in which you manage the pressures of employment as well as making time for other important areas of your life. Although this is not the main focus of this chapter, it may be useful to consider how you intend to manage your time in the future. You may have some experience of this from your current studies – perhaps completing a study timetable, for example. If so, time management can be regarded as the type of transferable skill considered earlier.

PRACTICAL TASK

From your university or local library, find a book relating to time management that you can read. If you are able to, you may wish to use Getting organised *(Thody and Bowden, 2004). The reference for this is listed at the end of the chapter.*

Knowing the limits of your responsibility

Thompson and Thompson (2008) refer to the CIA model as a method of reducing personal or work-based pressure. They suggest that there are some situations that can be 'controlled' ('C'), some that cannot be controlled but can be 'influenced' ('I') and others that can neither be controlled nor influenced and must therefore simply be 'accepted' ('A'). Using this model can create a sense of perspective about the amount of control that a person has in any situation, and may assist when dealing with frustration. It may therefore be useful to consider incorporating the CIA model into your reflections where appropriate, perhaps following a situation that you found stressful or frustrating.

REFLECTIVE TASK

Think of a recent situation that you found frustrating. This may have been something from your personal life, or perhaps something during your studies. Practise reflecting upon it using Borton's (1970) model. When answering the 'What?' question, also consider the amount of control or influence that you feel you had in the situation. Was there anything that you had to simply accept?

If you feel confident enough, you may prefer to use Gibbs's (1988) reflective cycle – you might use the questions highlighted earlier. Include the CIA model when considering 'What more could have been done?'

Making the most of appraisals: the Performance and Development Review (PDR) process

Most employers require their staff to take part in some form of annual appraisal. This term refers to the assessment of an individual's performance, and usually takes place on an annual basis. In many organisations, including the police service, these are referred to as Performance and Development Reviews. More detailed information can be obtained by visiting the 'Workforce Strategy' section of the National Policing Improvement Agency (NPIA) website.

Visit the 'Workforce Development' section of the NPIA website. The web address is provided here: **www.npia.police.uk/en/7919.htm**.

Open and read the section entitled 'National PDR System'. Make a list of the reasons that you think that your annual appraisal or PDR may assist your development.

PDR and police improvement

A key reason for the use of a PDR system is that it allows an organisation to ensure their staff have the correct skills for the role that they perform. For the police service, the standard of staff performance is measured against a series of competencies that are agreed at national level. By doing this it is possible to ensure that all policing staffs are competent within their role, and that the service continues to develop and improve. This, as discussed earlier, relates to the requirement that modern employers and their staff are committed to lifelong learning.

During your future role, it is therefore likely that you will be required to engage in an annual review of your performance with your line manager. This is so that your objectives for the previous period can be evaluated and new ones can be set for the forthcoming year. There are a variety of things that you may be required to demonstrate in order to have completed your appraisal objectives; a few are listed here.

- An understanding of a particular system or policy.

- A specific type of skill – communication, for example.

- Participation in a particular training event, such as health and safety.

Here, we consider the ways that within the PDR process you can use a reflective approach to engage as a way of assisting your own development.

Reflecting on the PDR process

Appraisals provide a useful opportunity to reflect upon your performance because they are designed to provide specific feedback for you. Most academic institutions require students to take part in a similar type of performance development programme. You may therefore already be accustomed to monitoring your own progress. Equally, it is likely that you are developing the ability to use and reflect upon feedback, either informally from your peers and tutors or formally from assessed assignments. This ability is therefore a transferable skill that can be used to assist your development in the future. During your career it may be useful to use your reflective time in order to consider the following areas.

- The feedback you have received during a PDR or appraisal.

- The implications of it for your performance and development – in other words, your assessment of its meaning. What are your strengths and weaknesses, and might they cause any difficulties for your performance or even promotion?

- The objectives that have been agreed and how you intend to achieve them. These may be recorded as part of your appraisal; alternatively, you may wish to make a personal action plan in your diary as part of your ongoing reflections.

Reflecting for appraisal

The above approach to your appraisal may be useful in a variety of ways. It can, for example, allow you to take a structured approach to your career development. Importantly, however, reflection may also be used in order to provide evidence of your progress for future appraisals. This may take the following forms.

- The ability to explain clearly what your development has been.

- The evidence of reflections recorded within your diary.

- A portfolio containing evidence of your progress and development.

Constructing a portfolio

Here, we briefly consider the value of compiling a professional portfolio. You may already have had some experience of developing a learning portfolio during your current educational programme. Jasper (2003) suggests that within the healthcare professions, practitioners are often required to provide evidence of their continuing professional development. Some, such as registered nurses, may be unable to re-register for practice unless they have done so. It usually takes the form of a portfolio containing a collection of documents. These demonstrate that the practitioner has taken an active role in developing and improving their skills and knowledge. There is a danger, however, that this may simply become a folder that contains a pile of certificates from the courses that have been attended. A comprehensive professional portfolio may include the following types of evidence.

- A personal statement about yourself, your future ambitions and your attitude towards your work.

- A current curriculum vitae.

- A copy of your most recent PDR.

- An action plan for future development.

- A list of your transferable skills.

- A record of courses and educational programmes that have been attended.

- Some written reflections upon your learning from the above events, and how it might be applied in order to assist your professional performance.

- Some pages from your diary that demonstrate your ongoing professional reflections.

It should be stated, however, that while diaries are an effective method of demonstrating a reflective and lifelong learning approach to your development, they should avoid disclosing any sensitive material relating to yourself or others, such as colleagues or members of the public.

This type of professional portfolio is not currently a requirement for police officers; however, you may wish to consider developing something similar in the future. Doing this may help you to stand out as a member of staff that takes an organised approach to their development. Your portfolio may be presented as additional evidence for your PDR or, indeed, for a future promotion. We consider this in the final section of the chapter.

Future promotion

As a student, it may feel strange to be asked to think about your promotion in what seems like the distant future. It is possible that you have already considered the type of policing role that you wish to pursue. Indeed, you may also have some idea of the level of promotion you would like to achieve. Alternatively, however, you may feel less clear about the future at this stage, and wish only to complete your studies successfully.

The most important thing to be aware of is that adopting a reflective approach to your development can assist you in planning a successful career. This may relate to your continued development within a particular role or to planning future promotion. Many of the techniques already discussed can assist you in taking an ambitious approach to climbing the career ladder. These are summarised here.

- Regularly reflecting upon practice.

- Recording reflections in a diary.

- Completing action plans.

- Engaging in the PDR process.

- Compiling a reflective portfolio.

Finally, we briefly consider some additional strategies that may be used when planning future promotion. These include developing an awareness of the options and assessing your transferable skills.

PRACTICAL TASK

Complete the following two tasks.

1 Using either one of your existing textbooks about policing or a book from the library, explore the various ranks within the policing structure. You may already have an understanding of this from your studies. If so, make a list in order to refresh your memory.

2 Visit the website for a police force of your choice. You may consider the one nearest to you or perhaps the force that you wish to apply to in the future. Explore the website in order to gain an understanding of the types of specialist role that are available.

Exploring the options

An important element of promotion planning is developing an awareness of the future opportunities. As discussed, you may already have a clear idea about this, or this may develop as your career progresses. It may be that you wish to progress through the ranks of policing, for example, or you may choose to pursue a particular policing speciality. Your annual appraisal may provide an opportunity to discuss these types of opportunities with your line manager.

Transferable skills

In the same way that transferable skills may be used in order to assess your employability, they can also be used to demonstrate your suitability for a promotion or a specialist role. It is possible, therefore, to use future reflection to assess the following.

- The skills that you have developed.

- The types of role that are most compatible with these skills.

- The skills needed for a particular role.

- The measures that you can take in order to acquire these skills.

You may therefore choose to write an action plan within your reflective diary or set a range of targets during your PDR in order to achieve these goals.

PRACTICAL TASK

Knowledge check review

On a piece of paper, or perhaps in your reflective diary, revisit the questions completed at the start of the chapter. Compare your answers in order to assess your learning.

- *What do I know about the importance of lifelong learning for my future career?*

- *What do I think the term 'employability' means?*

- *What type of skills am I developing for future employability?*

- *What can I remember about reflecting 'on' and reflecting 'in' action?*

- *How might they help me improve my practice as a future police officer?*

- *What do I think a Performance Development Review might involve?*

- *How might reflection help me to plan and achieve promotion in the future?*

C H A P T E R   S U M M A R Y

This chapter has considered the uses of reflection during various stages of your future career development. It has explored the role of lifelong learning for career development. The chapter then considered the use of reflection for assessing your employability. Finally, an exploration of the uses of reflection for professional development and promotion was provided. You should now have a fuller understanding of how reflective practice can assist you in planning a successful career.

FURTHER READING

Thody and Bowden (2004) *Getting organised* provides a pocket-sized introduction to managing various aspects of student studies, including time management. These can easily be considered in the context of professional development.

REFERENCES

Bingham, R and Drew, S (1999) *Key work skills*. Aldershot: Gower Publishing.

Borton, T (1970) *Reach, touch and teach*. New York: Mcgraw-Hill.

Dacre Pool, L and Sewell, P (2007) The key to employability: developing a practice model of graduate employability. *Education and Training*, 49 (4): 277–89.

Fullick, L (2004) *Adult learning in a brave new world: lifelong learning policy and structural changes since 1997*. Leicester: National Institute for Adult Continuing Education.

Gibbs, G (1988) *Learning by doing: a guide to teaching and learning methods*. Oxford: Oxford Polytechnic.

Home Office (2002) *Training matters*. London: Home Office. Available online at http://webarchive. nationalarchives.gov.uk/+/http://www.homeoffice.gov.uk/hmic/training_matters.pdf (accessed 27 October 2010).

Jasper, M (2003*). Beginning reflective practice*. Cheltenham: Nelson Thornes.

Morgan-Klein, B and Osborne, M (2007) *The concepts and practices of lifelong learning*. London: Routledge.

O'Dowd, D (1999) *Managing learning: a thematic inspection of police training*. London: HM Inspector of Constabulary.

Payne, E and Whittaker, L (2006). *Developing essential study skills*, 2nd edition. Harlow: Prentice Hall.

Spurling, A (1995) *Towards an unknown land: lifelong career development into the future*. West Sussex: Hobson Publishing.

Thody, A and Bowden, D (2004) *Getting organised*. London: Continuum.

Thompson, S and Thompson, N (2008) *The critically reflective practitioner*. New York: Palgrave Macmillan.

USEFUL WEBSITES

http://cfnp.npia.police.uk (National Policing Improvement Agency)

www.policecouldyou.co.uk/ (Could You? Police recruitment website)

Index